Letter to My Children

Letter to
My Children

*From Romania to America
via Auschwitz*

Rudolph Tessler

University of Missouri Press

Columbia and London

Copyright © 1999 by
The Curators of the University of Missouri
University of Missouri Press, Columbia, Missouri 65211
Printed and bound in the United States of America
First paperback printing, 2024

Library of Congress Cataloging–in–Publication Data

Tessler, Rudolph.
    Letter to my children : from Romania to America via Auschwitz /
Rudolph Tessler.
        p.   cm.
    ISBN: 978-0-8262-1244-3 (hardcover); 978-0-8262-2322-7 (paperback alk. paper)
    1. Tessler, Rudolph. 2. Jews—Persecutions—Romania—Vişeu de
Sus. 3. Holocaust, Jewish (1939–1945—Romania—Vişeu de Sus
Personal narratives. 4. Tessler, Rudolph. 5. Vişeu de Sus
(Romania)—Ethnic relations. 6. Holocaust survivors—Illinois
Biography. I. Title.
DS135.R72V577   1999
940.53' 18' 094984—dc21   99–35479
                                                                        CIP

☉ This paper meets the requirements of the
American National Standard for Permanence of Paper
for Printed Library Materials, Z39.48, 1984.

Text design: Stephanie Foley
Jacket design: Mindy Shouse
Typesetter: Crane Composition
Printer and binder: Thomson-Shore, Inc.
Typeface: Granjon

Rabbi Akivah lived at the time of the Bar Kochva rebellion against Rome. He was a shepherd until he reached the age of forty, when he met Rachel, the beautiful daughter of Calba Savua, the richest man in Jerusalem. Rachel told Akivah that she would marry him if he would go to study Torah and give up being a shepherd. He agreed. Secretly they married. When her father learned of the marriage, he disowned her, and the couple lived in poverty.

Akivah did what Rachel had asked him to do and went away to study. After twelve years he returned, accompanied by twelve thousand students. Rachel's neighbors were talking with her, asking how long she would live and behave like a widow. "Your husband has left you; he has forgotten you," they said. "How long can you go on like this?" She replied that if it were up to her, she would not mind if he was to learn for twelve more years.

Akivah learned of that conversation. He went away and came back twelve years later. This time he was accompanied by twenty-four thousand students. The throngs were welcoming him. Among them was his wife, who was trying to reach him in order to kiss his feet. The students tried to push her away. When Akivah saw that, he said to the students: "For all that I am and all that you are, it is because of her."

My accomplishments belong to my wife, Edith. All that I am and all that my children are is because of her. She has been the anchor, the beacon, and the compass of our family. Were it not for my wife's encouragement and support in all my endeavors, I would not have been able to accomplish what I did and what I do, and my children and I would not be what we are.

In every phase of our marriage, the running of our house and the taking care of our children, without her having a mother and father to guide and help her bring up the children, with meager resources, and without ever complaining, she showed the inner strength that she has in great abundance. She always was at my side when times were difficult, as well as when they were easier. She is the role model for our children and our extended family.

King Solomon describes "a Woman of Valor" and enumerates the virtues she should possess. Edith possesses all of them.

It is for my dear wife that this book is dedicated.

It also is dedicated to the thousands of victims from my town of Viseu, Romania, and Edith's town of Papa, Hungary, who perished without leaving behind any family members or anyone to remember them. May their memories be blessed, and may the Almighty avenge their blood.

Contents

Preface ix

A Way of Life 1

The Coming Darkness 30

The Train Turned North to Auschwitz 53

Prisoners in Warsaw 64

A Death March to a Death Train 74

Dachau and Muhldorf-Waldlager 81

The Last Mad Days 110

Liberated 133

Aftermath 140

To Viseu and Back 159

Restless 179

In America 195

Return to Viseu 212

Conclusion 225

Preface

For many years I have been encouraged by my children, their spouses, and my friends to write about my experiences. For many years I have resisted.

The Psalms say that the life span of a person is seventy years. If a person is exceptionally worthy, it can be eighty years. I have reached three score and ten years. The fiftieth year after liberation of the German concentration camps came a few years ago, with many commemorative activities taking place. I decided it was time to record my experiences.

There is a Jewish tradition of remembering. Going back thousands of years, G-d commanded Moses, "Always remember Amalek." Amalek was the first nation to persecute the Jews after the exodus from Egypt. "Remember what they did to you. They tried to destroy you when you were leaving Egypt." In fact, there is a Sabbath that is called the Sabbath of Remembering. It is Parshas Zachor, and its purpose is to remember what your enemies have done to you.

Our tradition also tells us not to hate for the sake of hating. We have to remember what the Egyptians did to us when our forefathers were slaves there. But we do not hate the Egyptians. For so many years the Jews dwelt in Egypt but, even though they were slaves, we have to remember that they were sheltered there and grew into a nation.

There have been other reasons for me to write. I want to describe how life was before the Second World War in the part of the world where I was brought up, a place that no longer exists for Jews. While there was no great wealth, there was spiritual happiness. The people respected their parents, their elders, and their spiritual leaders. Life revolved around one's family and the community. Sabbath and holidays were full of happiness and joyful celebration. During those days a German tourist wrote that the Jews he saw leaving the synagogue after the Sabbath service in our town were the happiest people he had ever seen.

In the past sixty years the rest of the world also has greatly changed. I have experienced many of these changes. During this time our people have gone through violent and tragic times. Never in the history of the world did any people suffer as much in such a short period of time.

The world has changed in many scientific and technological ways. In transportation it has gone from primitive carts to jet travel. In communications it has changed from writing letters and sometimes waiting weeks for them to be taken from place to place, to instantaneous transmissions of voices, pictures, and messages of all kinds.

At the same time, in many ways the world has not progressed. We clearly have gone backward in terms of moral and ethical behavior and in the decline of the family as the most important part of our lives. There is no respect for elders or religious leaders. Without question, this has been the most barbaric century in history, including the attempt to destroy an entire people because of their religion.

Another reason for writing is that I have read many books about the happenings of the Holocaust and have seen that they contain many errors. I am compelled to write because I know what actually happened. I was there. I saw with my own eyes.

Most of those books tell of the physical sufferings and the heroism of the victims and the survivors. Very little, however, has been written about the moral and spiritual strength that enabled people to survive. If it were not for that, no one would have been able to survive.

I am one of the few who survived with a father. In almost all instances, fathers and sons were separated and one or the other was killed for being too old or too young. I also am one of the youngest survivors.

As I write these words, so much is still too difficult to comprehend. How I could experience so much suffering and remain sane is a miracle in itself. Sixty-seven members of my family—my mother, her father, my three sisters, three of my brothers, aunts, uncles, and cousins—were murdered at Auschwitz.

My two brothers and I are the last of our generation, the generation that shared a way of life that had been experienced for hundreds of years. I witnessed the total destruction of that way of life. I subsequently experienced the rebuilding of our lives, the founding of the state of Israel, and the revival of Judaism.

As time goes on, it will become increasingly difficult to recall the details of what happened. That is why it is critical for me to write now before my memory may begin to fail and the experiences fade. Happily, I am fortunate that I am blessed with a good memory.

For all these reasons I have decided to tell my story as I lived it to enable my children, my grandchildren, and future generations to know where we came from, who we were, what we experienced, and what we have accomplished despite the suffering. I want my children, my grandchildren, and all who come after them to know from me firsthand what happened.

Letter to My Children

A Way of Life

My father's name was Salomon. My mother's name was Esther. My brothers and sisters were Buroch, Mendel, Golda, Hersh, Fradel, Shmiel Chaim, Toba Gitel, and Yehuda Meir.

We, the rest of our family, and the people from our part of the world once had a way of life. I would like to leave a record of those people, the way they lived, the way they earned their livelihoods, the way they shared and helped each other, before everything was destroyed.

I was born October 13, 1926, in northern Romania in Viseu-de-Sus, a town nestled in the foothills of the Carpathian Mountains in a region known as Marmaros. Political control over Marmaros changed frequently. Prior to the end of World War I, it was part of Austria-Hungary. When that empire was defeated in the war, Marmaros was divided between Romania and Czechoslovakia. In 1940, during the Second World War, it was occupied by Hungary. It was an area over which there was continuing dispute.

My family was part of a thriving, spiritually rich Jewish culture. For almost two centuries we had the good fortune to have famous rabbis in the local synagogues. Many would go on to become important rabbinical leaders around the world. A small number of Jews had lived in northern Romania since the early eighteenth century. Most of them were poor, living in villages and subsisting on what they could grow on the small plots of land they were allowed to own. Some were storekeepers who sold supplies to the Romanian farmers. Like their

1

neighbors, most of these Jews were uneducated and lived a grinding, difficult existence in a primitive region where few had much money or land. Only the members of the landed aristocracy and certain businessmen were relatively well off.

Around 1750, three brothers were sent to the region by the Bal Shem Tov, the founder of Hasidism, to be spiritual advisers and teachers to the Jews who were living among the Romanians. The brothers transformed Jewish life in Viseu and the surrounding area. They were named Fruchter, Stern, and Adler, names given to them by the Austrian Emperor Francis I during a hunting trip to this remote part of his kingdom. The emperor, and many other hunters and visitors as well, were attracted by the area's wild natural beauty and also by Valea Vinelui, a famous resort at a mineral springs about six kilometers from my hometown. But there were no inns or hotels, so the emperor stayed in the house of one of the brothers. Before he left, he gave the brothers German names: Fruchter, because that brother was a fruit merchant; Stern, or "star," because he was bright and knowledgeable; and Adler, or "eagle," because he traveled widely, obtaining various provisions that he supplied to the Austro-Hungarian army, and thus saw a bit more of the world than most. It was the brothers' mission to bring the joy and learning of the Hasidic way of life to the Jews who lived in such poor conditions. The warmth of the traditions and learning of this movement changed the lives of our people dramatically and wonderfully. We grew enriched by learning and faith, not by money and possessions.

In the smaller towns of Marmaros, but not in the larger ones, most of the Jews became Hasidic. Hasidic Jews differed from other Jews in their garb and their belief of a more spiritual and emotional religion. They believed that you cannot ask G-d to explain your way of life. They believed that the way to come to G-d is by being happy, by worshiping G-d without asking any questions and without understanding Him, because you will never be able to fully understand Him. They believed in spontaneity, in warmth, in being intimate with G-d, not ritualistic and formal. One does not necessarily need to understand all of G-d's actions in order to plead with Him. G-d knows what He is doing and you are not to question His actions. One should be happy at all times regardless of one's material possessions or lack of them.

The Hasidic rabbis taught that you can reach G-d without being learned, that you can become pious and can pray to G-d and be heard without the benefit of great learning. This was an appealing message to a poor Jew in a small village where there was no rabbi, no teacher, nobody to teach him more than the basic alphabet and how to read.

In Jewish law, in order to pray there must be a minyan, a gathering of at least ten male Jews of age thirteen and older. Often, there were not ten in a village. So there were many Jews who had to travel to larger towns to pray on the special holidays. It was to these Jews of the villages that the Hasidic movement said you can become pious just by observing and by practicing and, gradually, you will learn. Thus the Hasidic rabbis taught the Jews the basics, what one must do to be an observant Jew.

In the eighteenth century, the learned Jews were in France and Germany, not in the small villages of Eastern Europe. The majority of the Jews in Eastern Europe had primitive educations. But gradually, the Hasidic Jews established educational institutions. Some small villages had rabbis who were learned men and great scholars, rabbis who were totally unselfish and attracted students from distant areas. Some villages even had great yeshivas, or schools. As a consequence, the people became more educated. Secular education, however, was considered unimportant and unnecessary.

Fruchter, Stern, and Adler had helped to create communal organizations for the Jews. Prior to their arrival, Jewish communal life in our part of the world was nonexistent. Soon the brothers became the so-called rich people of the area. I am a descendant of Fruchter.

I was the oldest of nine children, three girls and six boys. My name was Naftali. How it came to be Rudolph is a part of this story that I will get to later.

My father, Salomon, was the second-youngest in his family of eight boys and two girls. They were Shmuel Yehuda, Mendel, Berel, Yitzchok, Pinchus, Faiga, Yenta, Leib, my father, and Buroch. Berel died in the First World War. Five of the brothers emigrated to the United States before the turn of the century. The last of my father's brothers left in 1898, the year he was born. My father and his brother Buroch stayed in Viseu. Faiga, their sister, lived nearby in Moisei, and their sister Yenta lived in the town of Borsa.

My mother, Esther Rosenfeld, came from the portion of Marmaros that became part of Czechoslovakia. Like my father, she was from a large family. She was a warm, outgoing woman, very beautiful, tall, well-dressed. She was a great household manager, a wonderful cook, and an excellent baker.

My mother was of strong character. She was the leader of her brothers and sisters. She had run my grandfather's business, and she would help my father in his. When she came to live in Viseu she became a very prominent person. People looked up to her. In married life, my mother became a renowned housekeeper. Even during the war years, when it was difficult to get food, we never had a shortage. She always was able to get what she needed.

Her oldest brother was married to a woman from Viseu. That woman's family introduced my mother to my father. My father used to tell us that when her oldest brother was married, my mother was there as a baby. My father was at the wedding because it was customary for the whole town to participate. He said that he stole my mother, his future bride, from the cradle. My father was six years older than my mother.

My mother and father were married in 1925 when he was twenty-seven years old. You might call him a late starter. During World War I, when he was seventeen, he was in the Austro-Hungarian army. He finished the war in the Tyrolean area of Italy. After the war he refused to eat cucumbers because for months, while his unit was isolated in the Italian woods, all they had to eat was cucumbers, wild nuts, and chestnuts. After he was discharged at the age of nineteen, he began to study the Talmud seriously. He was a very learned man.

I was the oldest male grandchild who lived in our town. There were older grandsons but they did not live there. A male child or grandchild was valued more than a daughter or a granddaughter in Viseu, just as in many other areas and cultures. And I was spoiled.

I remember both my paternal grandmother, who died in 1936, and my grandfather, who lived until 1943. My paternal grandmother's name was Fradel Traubkatz Tessler. She came from the family of Cohanim (or "priests"). My paternal grandfather's name was Mordecai Tessler, but he was known as Mottel. He was a short man who wore a long coat with pockets that always seemed to be filled with candy. The children in our town liked to mill about him, sticking their hands into those pockets for candy whenever they wished.

My maternal grandmother, whose name was Golda, died shortly after World War I during the influenza epidemic then rampant in much of that part of the world. As a result, my mother, who was the oldest unmarried daughter, became her family's housekeeper and hostess.

Prior to 1920, my mother's town, Vilchovitz, was in Austria-Hungary, and no border separated it from Viseu. But with the defeat of the Austro-Hungarian Empire at the end of the First World War, Marmaros was divided into two parts. The area south of the Tisa River was annexed to Romania, and the area to the north became part of the new nation of Czechoslovakia. After the Treaty of Versailles, travel between the two towns required a passport and everything that crossing borders entailed. Still, every summer my mother and her two oldest sons—I being the older of the two—went to visit my maternal grandfather in Vilchovitz.

Near Vilchovitz was the town of Tecs, where my grandfather was born. My great-grandfather had run away to Tecs to escape being drafted into the Russian army. This happened sometime before 1830. The town that he fled from was Rzeszow, located in what was the Polish part of Russia. In those days, the Jews who lived in Poland and Ukraine lived in small towns, and the towns belonged to the landed aristocracy. No Jews were allowed to reside in the towns at that time except those who were needed by a baron to teach his children, to make shoes for him, to make horseshoes, or to perform some other specific skill that he wanted. Always there had to be a needed skill. My great-grandfather was the first Jew who received permission to live in Tecs without a specific role, trade, or skill. His name was Naftali Diamond, and at a young age, about thirteen, he left his family and went to live in Tecs with the Rosenfeld family, who had been given special permission to be in Tecs because the father was a tailor. Later my great-grandfather took Rosenfeld as his family name.

Subsequently, Naftali married my great-grandmother, Esther. They had six children. Shmiel Chaim, my grandfather, was the oldest. Next was Leibish. Then, Genendel and Moishe. Moishe became prominent. He was rich and famous because he was able to keep people out of the Austro-Hungarian army. He was, for lack of a better word, a fixer. His success was not due to bribes but to the techniques he used. He told the young men how not to pass muster when they came before the doctors. As a result, they were deferred. At the end of the war, because he had kept most of the boys from being drafted, he was put in jail. His work was not considered legitimate, but then, in the dismembered Austro-Hungarian Empire, nothing was legitimate.

Earlier, if my great-grandfather had not run away, he would have been in the Russian army shooting at a brother in the Hungarian army. The boundaries were always changing, and the governments kept drafting men as they were needed. There was no such thing as signing up with a draft board when you were such and such an age. You were literally grabbed off the street and thrown into the military. Many years later I met some people who had spent many years in Siberia simply because they had not been lucky. You see, it was not a question of evading the draft; it was one of survival.

My great-uncle was not called Rosenfeld. His nickname was Moishe Tecser because he was from Tecs and he was well known in the whole area. To this day, people from that area still remember him. Many times he came to our town to visit with us. He died in 1939.

Another of my great-grandparents' children was Feivish. The name of the other girl I do not remember.

My grandfather Shmiel Chaim was a great leader in the Viznitz Hasidic movement and very prominent in his town. His whole life was devoted to the Viznitz Hasidic movement. He owned land and a tavern. When he prayed, especially on Sabbath, no one could stand near him. It was G-d and him. He was a tall, handsome man, very distinguished and authoritarian, very warm, outgoing and friendly, a very learned man. Because of his devotion to the Rabbi of Viznitz, he traveled from his town, which was in the Slovakian part of Austria-Hungary, to Viznitz, in the empire's Polish part. This was a great distance by horse-drawn carriage over intimidating mountains. He traveled to be with the Viznitz Rabbi for the High Holidays. He left his family for six to eight weeks.

My grandfather died in May of 1944. At the age of eighty-seven, he was taken to Auschwitz and murdered in the gas chamber, on the same day that my mother, who was forty-three, and six of my younger sisters and brothers, from fourteen to four years old, were also murdered.

Marmaros, with its wild environment and long winters, tested one's resourcefulness and strength. The mountainous, heavily forested terrain held very little level land suitable for farming. Given the short, intensely hot summers and the poor soil, farmers could raise only potatoes, or small amounts of corn, oats and vegetables that could survive in colder months. There were also beautiful orchards of apples, pears, and plums; fruit that was shipped to and sold in other parts of the country. The first snow usually fell in October and remained on the ground until March. The roads were dirt, and there were no sidewalks. In the winter the transportation was by sled, either horse-drawn or pulled by people.

It is hard to convey how isolated and primitive Marmaros was, even well into the early years of this century. Few people had much formal education, and most lacked culture and refinement. Their knowledge of the world beyond their forests and mountains was limited. The harshness of the environment forced people to depend on each other. The small farms around Viseu were cultivated by horse- and oxen-drawn plows and worked by hand. The limited productivity of such farms made communal cooperation essential. What little could be grown locally was soon consumed. Food was, accordingly, always in short supply, and little was wasted.

Most of the farmers were Romanians; a few were Hungarians. There were also numerous Germans living in the region, the Volksdeutsch or Swaben-Zipzern, as they were called, who had settled in the area centuries before. The Jews were found mainly in the towns, villages, and the few cities. The largest city in the area was Sighet, which had a population of twenty-five thousand and was located forty kilometers from Viseu.

The local economy was heavily based on lumber produced from the vast forests, a resource that attracted timber merchants from other parts of Europe. Those who cut down the trees had to pay the government for the right to do so. The Germans were the loggers and workers in the timber business. The few wealthy people in Marmaros, apart from the nobility, were those who owned sawmills and traded in timber. The other major source of income came from the importation of grain from other, more fertile parts of the country. The Jews played an important part in this trading activity.

In my town, Viseu, the population was about one-third Romanian, one-third German, and one-third Jewish, with a small number of Hungarians. The Germans in town were Catholics. Most of the Romanians were Romanian Orthodox; some were Catholics of the Eastern Rite. On national holidays a Catholic priest and the rabbi made appearances together at public gatherings.

In 1941, there were almost five thousand Jews living in Viseu, or 35 percent of the population. Every Jew in our town was Hasidic; all wore the dark Hasidic clothes. On Sabbath every married man wore a shtreimel (a fur-tail hat) and a kaftan (long black coat). The women wore long clothing, skirts down to their ankles, sleeves to their wrists. All the married men had beards. Some beards were shorter than others. The boys had side curls, peyos.

When I was growing up, transportation was by horse and buggy. There were no automobiles in Viseu, not a single one. There was no electricity until the 1930s. As for telephones, there were only three. One was in City Hall. Another was used by the police, and the third was in the post office. There was a rich, so-called noblewoman by the name of Pap Simon, and she may have had a phone. If you needed to make a call to another part of the country, you would notify someone at the post office and then wait a few days for your call to go through.

I remember that the first radio was brought to town in the early 1930s. Another means of communication was the train that came through the town every day. The train ran from Sighet to Borsa; there were two stops before it reached Viseu. It would arrive every evening on its way from Sighet and would stop on its return trip the following morning. This train, with only a few cars, was the connection to express trains that went to other cities in Europe and the greater world beyond.

Life in my town was quite primitive and uncomplicated. People went about their business in a simple way. Modern-day pressures did not exist. There were no rich people as such. Some were better off than others because they owned land, dealt in timber, or sold flour and groceries wholesale. There were no grand houses; most were quite modest, one story, and built of timber, with no running water, sewers, or electricity.

Ours was an average-size house. We had no bedrooms, no living room, and no dining room. There was one central room that might be called a multipurpose room. In the kitchen there was a table which, at night, was converted into a bed where two kids slept. No one slept alone except the baby, who slept in a cradle. The kitchen had a combination of a stove and an oven built into the wall of the house. In the lower part of it you baked, and on the upper part you cooked. It had several places for pots and pans. The fire was made with wood. The wood was bought by the carload and stored outside our house. There it was chopped into smaller pieces for use in the oven and stove.

In addition to the oven on the lower part of the stove, there was one on the upper left. There was a space on one side of the oven that was large enough for one fortunate person to use as a sleeping niche. How warm and cozy it was in winter!

The kitchen, with its table and chairs, was the room we lived in. The other room was where we ate and where there were closets. I don't know how we managed, but that was the way it was.

When we got older, we had another room that served as the summer kitchen. That was where some of us slept. That room also was a sukka, a little hut that Jews use during the eight-day holiday of Sukkot, which is after Rosh Hashanah and Yom Kippur. You opened up the roof and you put up some leaves and branches to commemorate the holiday of Sukkot, which celebrates the gathering of the harvest.

Outside we had a big courtyard in which we raised chickens. We had a barn, the top part of which was used to store hay. We kept a cow for milk. We also stored food and perishables in the barn, because it was the coolest place we had in those days when there was no refrigeration.

In the back of our yard we had a big garden with fruit trees, and each spring we planted cucumbers, radishes, tomatoes, potatoes, green beans, and other vegetables. During the week we ate mostly milk products, a lot of bread and potatoes, eggs, and whatever vegetables were in season. For our Sabbath meal we had fish, chicken, or meat.

Everything was kosher—in fact, every Jew in our town kept kosher and virtually everything people ate was homemade and kosher, with the exception of bread, which was bought from the bakery in town.

When electricity came to our house in the early 1930s, it was only sufficient for a lightbulb. There was no running water. There was a well across the street. You had to get water with a pail, and many times in the winter, when the water in the well was frozen, you would have to chop through the ice in order to lower the pail. When the weather was very, very hot, and you needed to keep something as cool as possible, you lowered it in a bucket and kept it in the well. That's the way we kept things from being spoiled in the summer.

The typical house in Viseu, including ours, was not lavish by any means, but you always had room for everybody. When my maternal grandfather came to visit us from Vilchovitz, he was treated like a king. My father turned his bed over to him and my grandfather sat at the head of the table. The respect that one had for elders was normal and natural. Closeness was a way of life for all the generations.

My family owned a general store that sold everything from eyeglasses to flour, sugar to kerosene. There were supplies for wagons, cloth, shoes, pots and pans—whatever saleable items my father might obtain when he went on purchasing trips.

The distribution of products was quite limited. Items manufactured in one part of the country were not available in other parts. One had to import in order to provide what was sought by customers in our town. Fruits and vegetables that grew in other parts of Romania had to be found and shipped quickly to ensure that they arrived before they spoiled. My father was very resourceful in finding goods that our town needed. During the summer months he traveled to the fruit-producing areas of Romania and Hungary to find sellers of peaches, grapes, melons, etc. He would then hire a wagon to bring the produce to our town. Later, during fall, he found suppliers of corn, cabbage, and other food products. Transportation had to be arranged and produce had to be sold quickly before it spoiled or needed storage.

During fall and winter my father traveled to areas where factories were located. He never knew what he would find. He traveled to Cernowitz, Arad, Brasau, Medias, Oreadea near the Romania-

Hungary border. These areas manufactured textiles, leather goods, household goods, shoes, etc. He also traveled to Czechoslovakia for silk fabric and shoes that were very cheap there and more expensive in our town. He was always home by Friday afternoon in time for the Sabbath.

I remember once he came home with a carload of pots and pans, before Passover. It was a great success; many families wanted new pots and pans for Passover. The price was probably right as well. Once my father came home with a wagonload of knitted brown fabric from which you made sweaters. He did not know what to do with it. My mother and father put their heads together and they decided to make a dress from it. My mother wore it. She was a very beautiful woman, and the dress looked great on her. Everybody wanted to have the latest fashion like my mother. Before long everybody in town wore a brown dress made from my father's cloth.

Before the onset of winter each year, the people in town bought their supplies, which included sacks of cornmeal, flour, and lots of cabbage. One had to lay in sufficient food to last through the harsh winters. A trip to the local store, using a horse or ox-drawn sled to get through the drifting snow, was no minor undertaking! For those people my father stocked wagon loads of merchandise.

The store that my father operated belonged to my grandparents and, before them, to my great-grandparents. We lived in the house next to that of my grandparents, which was where my Uncle Buroch and his family also lived. (It was customary for the youngest son in a family to take over the household and the responsibilities for his aging parents. Because Uncle Buroch was the youngest, he moved in.) Adjoining my grandparents' house was our store.

In the kitchen of my grandparents' house there was a window that looked out on our yard. We did not need a telephone. All we had to do was holler. We were constantly going back and forth from our house to my grandparents' house.

I remember that my Uncle Mendel also stayed at my grandparents' house. He was one of my father's five brothers who had gone to America in the 1890s, because making a living in Marmaros was so difficult. (The last of these brothers had left in 1898, the year my father was born. Years later, after the war and the camps, my father was welcomed in New York by Isadore, a brother he had never seen. My uncle was seventy-two and my father was fifty when they first met.) Uncle Mendel had been in New York, where he made money in the necktie business. He came back to Viseu to marry someone religious. His intention was to return to the United States after marrying. But he liked the simple life better than the one in the United States. He married a local girl from a prominent Jewish family and stayed in Viseu.

Our house was the last one in which a Jewish family lived, adjacent to the German section. From that point on, there were Germans. My father's main business was with those Germans because we were surrounded by them. We lived with them. Our neighbors across the street and all around us were German. The Romanians who came to my father's store were very few in number. When they had farm produce to sell, my father bought it, and when they needed supplies, such as oil, kerosene, cloth, or whatever, they bought from us. Our business with the Romanians, however, was minimal.

The way of doing business in those days was quite simple. You entered the store, you bought what you needed, and you signed a book. Every customer had a page in the book and each signed it. This was the record of what was purchased and what was owed by each customer.

During the summer, when all the German men were off in the forests doing logging work, my father purchased the items he was going to sell to the families that stayed home. The German women stayed home and worked the fields. The women received some money from their men during the summer. Sometimes, however, what they received were the employers' promissory notes, like IOUs. My father accepted those notes and later collected from the employers. That was the custom in that part of the world. Sometimes the maker of the notes went bankrupt. Then you lost all that was due you for your labor. Merchants holding those notes could not collect what was due them either.

When the men went to work in the spring, they usually received an advance from the people who hired them, primarily in logging work. They took these advances and gave us the money on account. Then in summer, when they received more money from their employers, they paid us more. They settled their accounts for the year when they came home about a month before Christmas. They bought on account and they paid on account. So the book was never clear.

In the 1930s, of course, Romania suffered from the worldwide depression. There was a moratorium on the payment of debts. That became a way of life. There was no banking in the rural areas and no form of credit other than the primitive one I have described. During this time, people paid only a small percentage of their old debts. A new book had to be started for new debts. My father, therefore, began keeping two sets of books. Each customer paid on the new book whatever he had to pay; if there was a balance left over from earlier debts that remained unpaid during the moratorium, he paid against the balance due recorded in the old book. My father was to take the two books with him to Auschwitz. They were the only records of his business. They were his bank account. His total wealth was in those two books.

Our relationship with the local Germans was very good. We never had any problems, never. They came to us, they bought from us, and we sold to them.

My mother baked cakes for our German neighbors for Christmas and other important occasions. Those same neighbors visited us frequently. In May of 1944, when our family was taken to Auschwitz, my mother was greeted by one of those neighbors' sons as we got off the train. "Hello, Esther," he said. He had become a committed Nazi and had volunteered as an officer in the SS.

My mother was very active in the family business. In the late 1930s, my father was drafted as a reservist for the Romanian army and, although he wasn't away long, my mother ran the business. In later years, when it became dangerous for a Jew with a beard to travel—and, like most Hasidic men, my father had a beard—my mother was the one who traveled from place to place. She purchased the merchandise for our store and she had to bribe the police. She had to pay bribes because everything was both legal and illegal for Jews. As long as you paid, it was legal. If no payment was made, it was illegal.

I remember one particular bribe incident in our town. The police in our region were called gendarmes. The one usually in charge was the equivalent of a sergeant, and he usually had two or three deputies working for him. The gendarmes were not paid much. Taking bribes was a way of making ends meet. The sergeant in our town used to come to our store every month to pick up what he believed he was entitled to. Once, however, my father said that he didn't want to give it to him. "I don't need you," he said, "and I don't want to give it to you." But the gendarme subsequently caused so much trouble that my father decided not paying was not worth it. "So let's pay him every month whatever he thinks he has coming," my father said, "so we can conduct our business the way everybody conducts business."

Romania was a thoroughly corrupt country. British and French companies controlled the telephone and telegraph systems, the postal service, and the Ploesti oil fields. Romania had a large amount of oil and great natural wealth, but it was sold to the highest bidder. There was corruption everywhere.

In our town, for example, it took about sixty years to build a road. The reasons it took so long were many, but they all added up to corruption. All of the regional governors were appointed by the national government rather than being elected. The governors sold the building materials that were intended for the road, and they kept selling them. Moreover, roads were constructed by people who were grabbed off the streets. Men were simply drafted for four weeks or so to work on a road.

It is ironic that the pervasive corruption in Romania was directly linked to a lack of anti-Semitism. The greater the corruption in one region, the less likely it would be for a Jew to encounter difficulties. In the Second World War, Romania would be the only Nazi-occupied or satellite country in Eastern Europe not to send Jews to concentration camps. Jews were only sent to Auschwitz from the part of Romania annexed by Hungary during the war. Romania was a place where everyone knew who had to be paid and how much was expected.

Leadership within the Jewish community was markedly different from that of the government officials. In my time the communal responsibilities were clear. There was a rabbi, and all responsibilities revolved around the rabbinical court. The rabbi was the authority. No one questioned him. He was authorized by the government to perform official marriages and to keep the birth records, which became official documents.

Our town, small though it was, was quite renowned for having great rabbis. Rabbis were named after towns, so the rabbi in Viznitz, Rabbi Hager, was called the Viznitz Rabbi. He was a great scholar, a teacher with a magnetic personality that attracted many students. You didn't call him by the name Hager—there could be many Hagers. It was the name of the town that distinguished the rabbi. You usually didn't even know his real name. It would be irreverent and disrespectful to call him that. You didn't use his family name out of respect. It showed respect to address him as the rabbi of his town.

The respect for great rabbis was universal, shown not just by the Hasidic Jews in our town but by the Germans, Hungarians, and Romanians as well. It was a custom in those days for the rabbis to visit their disciples, called chasidim, in different areas. In our area the people were the disciples of the Viznitz Rabbi who lived in Oradea. Every year or two this rabbi made a tour to see his disciples in the various towns. People came from the surrounding areas to show their respect and spend time with him, usually a week or ten days. This practice is still carried on with great rabbis in Israel and America.

If the rabbi was a renowned individual, where he came from did not matter. In any given area there would be disciples of a particular rabbi. It was a dynasty that continues today in Israel.

One rabbi in particular, Israel Hager, was considered a great rabbinic leader internationally. He was the father of the rabbi of our town. When he came to Viseu, everything came to a halt. He came on a special train that stopped at many places along the way. At each town there would be a celebration. People would drink slivovitz, eat a piece of honey cake, and wish each other Lechaim (good fortune). All of the town's citizens went out to see the rabbi, including the gentiles. People made all kinds of flags, ornaments, and other decorations. It was like having a wedding. People came from the smaller villages and every town to see him. When any other renowned rabbi came, the same thing happened. There would be a great celebration. In fact, the local government officials made it sort of a semi-holiday. They, too, came to pay their respects and make speeches for the occasion.

This way of life came to an end in 1938, when the German

Anschluss swallowed Austria and Hitler began to threaten other countries. In this terrible new era the rabbis were afraid to travel, and sometimes they were even beaten.

In Viseu there were several synagogues. Each of the different parts of town had its own. The major synagogue, in the center of town, was well known. It had an ark that was one of the most famous in the world. It also had famous murals, and the statues of two lions on the exterior made the building a landmark. Whenever visitors came to town, they would leave with vivid memories of the synagogue and those two lions.

Every Jew of substance in the community had a permanent seat in the synagogue, and whenever a member of his family went there, he sat in that seat. It was inherited from generation to generation. Whenever I went there, I sat in my grandfather's seat.

From where we lived to the center of town was about a half hour's walk, but there was a closer synagogue, a rented house that had been converted. The house belonged to a German family. It had been a synagogue as far back as I could remember. Then, in the 1930s, when the Germans became more openly anti-Semitic, the synagogue had to be moved to a different house, one that belonged to a Jew.

That neighborhood synagogue was convenient, but on major holidays we always went to the main one. It was to the neighborhood synagogue, though, that each Jewish man first went when he got up in the morning. There he said his prayers before he went to work. He made another visit each evening.

Every morning in our town the boys and girls went to Hebrew school. The school was called Cheder. Our school day started very early. At six in the morning, you were on your way and stayed until about 8:30. Then we went to public school until noon, at which time we had lunch at home and returned until about 4:30. Then it was back to Cheder.

I never went to the town's Cheder. Prior to having the private teacher, Nechemia Schechter, I learned with teachers in their homes for several years.

It was customary for learned people who might not have been successful in business to become teachers. They recruited students themselves, sometimes by talking to the parents, sometimes by the reputations they had as good teachers.

Classes were in the homes of the teacher, and children were the same age and learned the same subjects. There were about twelve to sixteen in a class. Some teachers were great, some mediocre, and some in between. We learned religious subjects, Torah, Mishna, Gemara. For secular subjects we attended public school.

Parents paid tuition directly to the teachers. The school term started one week after Passover and ended one week before Rosh Hashana. The next term was from one week after the holidays until one week before Passover. During Passover and during Sukkot the evaluating of the teacher and testing of the children went on. These were the so-called market days.

In the teacher's house we sat on wooden benches in front of tables with the teacher at the head of the table. Sometimes the teacher fell asleep. It gave us a chance to be mischievous, as most children are. Once when our teacher fell asleep, we glued his beard to the table with paraffin from the candles that we used for light. Then we lit the wick in the paraffin and set it on the table. The teacher woke up when he felt his beard being burnt, since it was glued to the table. Of course we were punished after he recovered.

I also remember that once during the summer, about July or August, when there was no public school, we told our teacher one Friday that we had to attend public school. We gave him some phony reason. It was a beautiful summer Friday. We wanted to play ball instead of going to school, and we arranged for a ball game. Suddenly, we noticed our teacher appearing. He confronted us, saying, "So this is the public school you have to attend." We were severely punished. On Friday we were usually dismissed at twelve noon. That day we did not go home at twelve. When it got very late, our parents sent someone to the school to find out why we were not home yet. We were kept there all afternoon without food, and when we got home we were punished again by our parents. We learned our lesson.

In the winter, the room where we had our classes was heated with wood. The wood was bought by the carload and chopped into smaller pieces, then it was fed into a stove. The teacher at times lacked money to purchase the wood and hire someone to chop it into smaller pieces. At such times there was no heat. We froze.

Later, we children went to the market where wood was being sold. We helped ourselves to some wood or we followed the wagon hauling the wood. We made sure that some wood would fall off the wagon, which we brought to school, and made a fire to warm ourselves. Of course, we told the teacher that we got it from woodsellers because they felt sorry for us that we had to learn in a cold room.

After four grades of public school, you were no longer compelled to attend. Then you spent the whole day in Hebrew school, beginning at about six in the morning. Sometimes you might come home for breakfast. Sometimes not. But you always came home for lunch and dinner and went back to school until about nine o'clock. We had a long day. We learned exhaustively and extensively.

On Friday there was no school after twelve o'clock. Again on Saturday there was no school. Friday you helped with chores until the start of the Sabbath. Saturday was spent in the synagogue and learning with our father, as well as with festive Sabbath meals. Every child had to help, and I, as the oldest one, always had more responsibility. From the age of eight on, there were many times when I was in the store selling to customers. Or, if we ran out of something, I would run to the wholesaler to get what was needed. I would watch people so they wouldn't steal—from time to time there would be kids doing some pilfering.

During those years my father was always looking for different businesses to make some extra money. Many times he bought the fruit of an orchard before it was ripe. The baroness—Pap Simon—owned two apple orchards. My father bought the fruit from those orchards in late July or early August when you could not tell how much the yield would be. But he was willing to take the risk. He was buying what we call today "futures." If the yield was good in September or October, you would make money. My father would buy the fruit early, hoping that there would be no storms and that it would not turn rotten. You also had to be able to pick the fruit before the rainy season began, bring it into storage, and sell it right away. My father sold whole carloads to buyers in Germany and Czechoslovakia.

Most of the time he was successful. Occasionally there was a disaster because the fruit was destroyed by an early frost or storms knocking it off the trees. When the time came to pick the fruit, everyone had to work. My father hired people to do the job. It was essential that the pickers make sure that the fruit was not bruised. After picking, the fruit had to be separated and packed in different boxes. There were plums and many types of apples. We slept in the fields at night so no one would steal the harvested fruit before it was shipped.

It took many days to pick the fruit, leave it in piles and pack it. The most successful season was when the fruit was sold immediately after it was picked. Otherwise it had to be stored until there was a customer. Because there was no refrigeration, wagons had to be hired to haul the fruit as quickly as possible for shipping, or to a cool cellar for storage. So the kids and everybody else worked, literally around the clock. We also bought plums and made a jelly known as "lekvar." You opened up the plums, threw away the pits, put the fruit in giant kettles with fires underneath, and stirred the fruit. It was a twenty-four-hour operation for one batch of jelly. People had to be hired to open up the plums and to stir the kettle.

The plums or other fruit that were spoiled were accumulated in large barrels and made into whiskey. We had a so-called unofficial moonshine still that produced the whiskey. I believe the gendarmes knew about it and tolerated it—for the right consideration. But the work was always done at night. So, in our way of life, there were all kinds of ways to make a living.

With his business ventures, my father had to do a lot of traveling. As for me, my first trip alone away from Viseu came in 1939 when I was twelve. It was a great adventure.

I was going to Sighet by train to get eyeglasses. I was going to see my uncle, who would take me to the place where I was going to get the glasses. I got up early in the morning and put on my good suit. My family escorted me to the train.

The train I rode arrived at a very large station—Romania had beautiful train stations. I got off, went up to the driver of a horse cart, and asked how I could get to the address I had. "Wait a minute," he said. "You're still in the station. Go outside and ask how you get to that address." So I went outside and found that my uncle lived not far from there. I went to his house and met my aunt, who took me to the eyeglass man. He examined me and said I needed glasses. "I can do one of two things," he said. "I can get glasses for you but I don't know how long it will take to get them ready and they will cost a lot of money. Or I can give you glasses in about half an hour which are slightly used but will work OK. They work for everybody." I got the glasses that were available quickly. They were slightly used, but very cheap. I would wear them until after the concentration camps when the lenses were broken. To get them involved only a two-and-a-half-hour trip, but for me it was a major adventure.

Travel to a city such as Sighet was a rare adventure for boys my age in Viseu. Parents were very hesitant about letting their sons go away when they were in their late teens. The danger was that in the cities, many became irreligious. There was an additional problem: when the young men were nineteen or twenty they were eligible for the draft. Money would be have to be paid to the state to avoid going into the army.

In my town, when Jews grew up, they either got married or went away to one of the big cities. Some went into business; others began peddling. Some went to be teachers in smaller villages; others went to learn trades in the big cities. The main trades were those of cabinet-maker, shoemaker, tailor, printer, pocketbook-maker, and jeweler. Few Jews went into the professions. Before the Second World War it was impossible for a Jew in Marmaros to become a doctor. For all practical purposes we had no high schools or colleges available. How could you become a doctor when there was a quota system? It was called "numerous clauses." The universities only admitted a certain number of Jews—only the administrators of the universities knew what the numbers were. You couldn't get into a medical school without fitting in under the right quota.

Moreover, there were no public high schools in the small towns. To attend one, you had to go to a big city. To afford that, you had to be rich. What is more, the teachers and the entire high school system were very anti-Semitic. The teachers were part of the elite. Romania had peasants and it had an elite, and the elite were the people in government. No matter which government was in power, the people in it were always the elite.

There were very few colleges and universities, and you just couldn't get into a medical school. I knew a man in our town who originally came from a small village and had to go to France to become a doctor. Another doctor from our town, a man slightly older than I, also had to go to France to study. Once, on his way there, he was thrown out of a train by anti-Semites.

The truth was that Romania did not allow Jews to become professionals. To become a doctor, an engineer, or any other professional in Romania was virtually impossible. People, however, became famous entrepreneurs. Quite a few became industrialists. Some were writers, some of whom changed their names. Before, during, and after the First World War many of the Jews from Romania went to France and Italy, and quite a few went to Argentina. In fact, in Argentina they came to control the leather industry. There is, of course, a lot of cattle there and, consequently, many leather products are produced. The industry was controlled by Jews who were from our area. Uruguay is another country to which Jews from Marmaros emigrated with much success.

Poland had Jewish members of parliament prior to World War II. They represented the heavily concentrated Jewish populations of the cities. Romania, on the other hand, had no such concentrations. So Jews could not elect their own. Democracy as such did not exist in Romania. It called itself a democracy, but it wasn't.

We continued in Hebrew school until we were twelve or thirteen. Then the children went to the Hebrew equivalent of high school. My father, however, was a very progressive man, and he arranged for my next oldest brother, Buroch, and me to have a private teacher in someone's house for a number of years, starting from when I was ten years old. My father and a neighbor, Mr. Fogel, who also sent his kids to this private school, paid for the teacher. The teacher (I have heard that he may still be alive and living in Israel) was Nechemia Schechter.

These classes took place in the home of one of the boys. Our teacher was in his twenties; therefore, he was of draft age. Every male of twenty or twenty-one had to go into the army, but Romania had an unusual practice. A rich man could buy a horse, supply it with food, and bring it with him to the army for only thirty days. After that, the man would be free to go, but the horse would belong to the army. My father and Mr. Fogel provided our teacher with the money for a horse in addition to his salary. That way he was able to continue almost un-interrupted as the teacher in our private Hebrew school. We contin-ued, along with other Jewish children in the town, to attend the communal Hebrew school, the Talmud Torah, but we were the only ones to have a private teacher.

I was taught by that teacher until I was eleven or twelve. Then I graduated to a yeshiva and studied there for about two years. Although Viseu was a small town, it was the site of the largest yeshiva in the world. It had a dormitory that could house close to four hun-dred boys. The yeshiva was headed by Rabbi Mendel Hager, a famous Hasidic rabbi, who was the uncle of the Rabbi of Viznitz in Bnei Braq, now a great Hasidic leader in Israel. In his time Rabbi Hager was con-sidered one of the most learned Talmudic scholars. In addition, he was an eloquent speaker. Twice a year he spoke in the great synagogue, once on Sabbath Teshuvah, which is the Sabbath after Rosh Hashanah, and once on Sabbath Hagodol, the Sabbath preceding Passover. When he spoke, he closed his eyes and spoke for exactly two hours and twenty minutes without any notes. He was a famous orator and was greatly respected all over the world. We were blessed to have this great and learned rabbi.

Rabbi Hager, who was known as the Viseu rabbi, traveled to America in 1936 for speaking engagements and to raise money for the dormitory in our town. Many thousands of people came to hear him in New York City and elsewhere. He was successful in raising money not only in the United States but also in Germany and other countries.

At public school, the Jewish boys were always best in scholastic achievement. The Romanians were the worst. Somewhere in between were the Germans. The Jews were always studying while the Germans were working with their hands, and the Romanians were usually working in their fields. The Romanians never really showed any interest in education. They went to school only because they had to. In the schools the Jews always did best. I should note that the school system was much more intensive than it is in America. When you graduated from an elementary school, you knew as much as today's college students in America.

The public schools had desks that sat two boys each. The best boys sat in the front rows of the classroom and the weaker students sat toward the back. My seatmate for a while was the son of the postmaster. His father asked me to help his son with the lessons. I agreed on condition that I got foreign stamps—I had a fine collection. Thus it came about that many letters in our town were delivered without stamps.

The Romanians and the Germans went into the army. Jews rarely did, only the poorer ones and only in the later years when the war winds were blowing. By then it was difficult not to go. But in the years before, Jews bought themselves out as often as they could, either by providing horses or by getting the community's help. If someone did not have the money, the community would come up with it. The army was thoroughly corrupt, as was Romanian bureaucracy in general. There was no great difficulty, therefore, in avoiding the army. The result was that the army was primarily composed of poor Romanians.

In our house my father used to test his children on what we had learned that week in school. This was normal. Even though I was young, I was still the oldest grandson of my grandparents living in town. My grandmother would give candy to all the children and especially to me. She would give me two pieces if I knew a subject well. If I didn't, there would only be one.

My father asked her how she knew how well I had mastered a particular subject. She said it was very simple. If the test went smoothly, then I knew. If it didn't go smoothly, then I didn't know. She gave me two pieces of candy because she said I would remember and say a prayer for her after her death. She favored me because she knew I would be carrying on generations and I would remember her at the anniversary of her death, called "yahrzeit."

Our way of life centered around the family. We may not have been rich financially, but we had spiritual richness, starting with our celebration of the Sabbath and continuing through all the holidays.

The Sabbath was the focal point for the Hasidic Jew. All week he struggled trying to earn a living and fulfilled his responsibilities as best he could. When Sabbath came, the house was clean, the children were dressed in their Sabbath clothes, and special foods were prepared. In fact, it was essential, whenever possible, to have meat, wine, and fish. We always saved the special foods for the Sabbath.

In addition, time was spent with the children. A father first tested his children on what they had studied during the week, then he taught them new subjects. On Friday nights and Saturday mornings we were in the synagogue for prayers. The Sabbath also was the time to visit family members, a time for the entire family to come together.

Holidays were special times with all the preparations and cleaning, getting supplies and clothes, and the celebration. A holiday was always a communal affair; everyone participated.

Passover was a major occasion, and so were Rosh Hashanah, Yom Kippur, and the Sukkot. We started to prepare for Passover as early as November because you could not just go to a store and buy the supplies you needed for it. Geese were bought in November and fattened over the winter until they were ready for slaughter. Arrangements had to be made with farmers to buy from them an egg at a time— there was no such thing as going to the store for a dozen eggs. You had to prepare wheat to make matzos, and the wheat had to be purchased in the fall and stored away so it wouldn't get soggy. You had to buy potatoes in the fall because they were cheaper than in the winter. You had to buy the onions and whatever additional supplies you needed. You also had to buy wine, but grapes did not grow in our area; it was necessary to travel elsewhere to purchase the wine and bring it home. So you had to think about such basic things and plan carefully over a long period of time. It was not easy.

All of this was done through joint ventures with neighbors.

This constant planning kept the Jews together—the celebrations and the communal responsibilities during times when people had very little money, or no money at all.

What we had, we shared. Everything was communal; the neighbors helped each other. When you wanted to build a house, it required seven or eight people. A man would do one thing and a woman would do another. Each person would contribute. The same was true in farming. When it was time for planting or harvesting, the neighbors would help with one field and then move on to another. In the same communal way we prepared for Passover. When the food was served, it was done on special Passover dishes. The dishes that had been used during the rest of the year could not be used on Passover. You were not allowed ones that had been used for bread products. These special Passover dishes were usually stored in the attic and had to be brought down.

For Passover, every boy and girl had to have a new suit, or a new dress and new shoes. A tailor used to come and take measurements— you didn't go to a store. The shoes, shirts, suits, and dresses were all custom-made. But many times the measurements did not result in clothes that fit properly or were made as ordered. Once when I was about eight, my mother wanted to give our business to a new tailor, one who had just advanced to journeyman. He forgot to allow for sleeves. But the suit he was making had a vest. So he took the vest and made sleeves from it. That was typical.

During the holidays we always celebrated in the synagogue, by going to visit each other, and by partaking in the delicious foods prepared by those we visited. If someone was in need, you never wanted to embarrass him. So you had to make sure that enough money was gathered for these events in such a way that no one knew where the money came from or to whom it went. This was the way of life.

There were certain communal leaders, like my father, the president of the Jewish community, and more prosperous people, who took responsibility. Nobody knew who gave, and nobody knew to whom money was given. It was the same in many other aspects of our lives. Often when a child was born and the parents had no money for a party, my father was the one who made sure the parents had what they needed.

The Jewish community was self-sufficient. It had a system of collecting revenue needed to meet the expenses of the community such as the salaries of the rabbi, Shochet (ritual slaughterer), Dayan (judge), sexton, teachers, and others, and to pay for the maintenance of important institutions such as the synagogues, schools, and mikvah.

When you needed to get animals ritually slaughtered, you had to buy a ticket from the community office. Then you took the ticket to where the slaughtering was done. This was in the courtyard of the community house where the Shochet lived. There was a little hut prepared for that. After the killing of a chicken, it was plucked of its feathers and taken home, where it was opened up. If a blemish was found inside the chicken, it was taken to the Dayan for his verdict as to whether it was kosher or not. There was a schedule of prices for slaughtering animals such as chickens, ducks, geese, and cattle. It cost more to slaughter a cow than a chicken, less for a duck than a goat. The community collected the revenues. The same was true for matzos for Passover. The community bought the flour, hired workers, added a small amount as a fee, and then sold matzos to the community. When one got married or when there was a funeral, a fee had to be paid to the community for services rendered. There were also communities that imposed a general tax, officially sanctioned and enforced by the government authorities.

Each synagogue was managed independently by its communities, but with its own bylaws, income, and expenses always subject and subservient to the authority of the rabbi of the city. The small surrounding villages were also subservient to the rabbi of our town. He was the rabbi of the entire region. Most villages had their own synagogues, mikvahs, and Shochet, but not a rabbi. The word of our rabbi was final. No one questioned his authority.

A wedding was a community affair. No invitations were sent. Everyone participated. The entire family. The entire town. There were no caterers. Everyone helped in preparing for the feast. There was no equivalent of today's large catering hall in which weddings are held. The house of the bride's parents, and that of a neighbor, would be cleared out. Men ate the wedding meal in one house, women in the other. The wedding ceremony took place in the communal courtyard, around which stood the small houses of the rabbi, the sexton, the Dayan, and the Shochet.

The Hasidic movement grew by leaps and bounds. Then, in the Second World War, much of it was destroyed. Today it is enjoying a great rebirth.

Before the storm clouds of the Second World War approached, life in our town was basically uneventful. Every summer we went to the Czech side of Marmaros to visit my maternal grandfather. We also visited the resort six kilometers from our town, Valea Vinelui. There we stayed in a cottage. One week my father would stay with the children and one week my mother would be there. They could not come at the same time because the store would have to be closed. The business had to go on. During those years before the war, the commerce of Romania continued to be conducted largely by the Jews.

Occasionally, we heard from my father's brothers in America. When they left in the 1890s, they were very poor. So were their parents, my grandparents. There was barely a way to make a living. So the sons picked themselves up and left.

One uncle had learned the knitting trade before he went to the United States. He was fourteen or fifteen at the time, and became a very rich man, the head of a knitting mill. Another uncle, a plumbing contractor in New York, also became wealthy.

My Uncle Sam returned from America to visit his parents in 1914, just before the First World War. The local people talked about how rich he was, so rich that he threw away all his children's cloth diapers when they were used. "Can you imagine that?" they said. "Can you imagine that Sam Tessler is so rich that he throws away diapers?"

Another uncle, Peter, returned to Romania in 1926 but left again just a month before I was born. My parents tried to persuade him to stay, telling him that he would be my godfather or something. But he said he had to go back. He had arrived in Viseu with a white straw hat and a white striped vest that he left behind, along with a cane. As kids, whenever we wanted to dress up, we played with the cane and the vest that Uncle Peter had left behind.

When Uncle Peter came to the Romanian border carrying a U.S. passport, he was told that he would have to pay. "What do you mean 'pay?'" he asked the border official. "I have a visa." The official said that he would decide who could enter, and Peter replied that he was going to contact the American embassy in Bucharest. "Do anything you want," said the official. "Go to the American embassy, go to Prague, go to America. Here you pay. You don't pay, you don't go through."

Uncle Peter had to pay. Otherwise, he would not have been allowed to cross the border. It was as simple as that.

Our family always wrote to my uncles in America. Occasionally my uncles sent some money home. Although my father was the second-youngest son in his family, he was the oldest one remaining in Romania. He received whatever money came from my uncles overseas, but he never used it. It was saved in case somebody in the family really needed it. I remember once when there was a five-dollar bill from one of my uncles. That was a great deal of money. One could live on five dollars for a long time.

So my parents had communication with my uncles. But in the early years my mother and father never had any intention to go to America. Later there would be no chance to go there.

People talked about America, but they were reluctant to leave our part of the world. Young people who left often became "modern"; they would assimilate and leave the fold of tradition. Some became nonreligious. That was the biggest concern about people leaving. It was also concern with those who left to learn a trade in one of the larger cities such as Sighet. Yet the people from our area had little concept of what America was all about. There were no movies. There was nothing visual to let you see America. All we knew came from letters, and what we learned was, in general, not good. So there was no great desire to go to America unless you were forced to emigrate.

It is true that in the 1880s and 1890s there had been movements to leave Marmaros to go to the United States, Argentina, and other places. Whole villages went to Minnesota and Connecticut. Others went to British-controlled Palestine. And in those days there were some rabble-rousers, agitators who went from town to town to encourage people to leave. But the 1920s and early 1930s were prosperous times in our part of Romania.

There had been other such prosperous times during the more than two hundred years in which Jews had lived in northern Romania. But there had been anti-Semitism as well. All of Eastern Europe and the Russian-dominated nations had periodic pogroms. Because of this, the Jews were constantly moving in an attempt to avoid brutal, systematic attacks by governments and gentiles alike. Czarist Russia was a particularly oppressive state. Some, such as Moses Mendelssohn in Germany, had argued that Jews should become assimilated with the people they lived among in order to escape oppression. The Hasidic rabbis disagreed. Assimilation would not help, they said. On the contrary, it would make matters worse. It would destroy the Jewish religion. That was the conflict of the times, and that was why the Hasidic movement had worldwide historic significance. It was created to protect Judaism.

Viseu was the only town in Marmaros that had a substantial German population. The next nearest area heavily populated by Germans was in south central Romania, closer to the Yugoslavian border. In the days of the Austro-Hungarian empire, there had been very little anti-Semitism in Marmaros, very little. It was bad in Ukraine, but not in Hungary and not in Romania. Ironically, the pervasive corruption in Romania was directly linked to a lack of anti-Semitism. The greater the corruption in one region, the less likely it would be for a Jew to encounter difficulties. Romania was a place where everyone knew who had to be paid and how much was expected. As a consequence, Romania would be the only Nazi-occupied or satellite country in Eastern Europe not to send Jews to concentration camps. Jews were only sent to Auschwitz from the part of Romania that was occupied and annexed by Hungary during the war.

Until the late 1930s, I had seen anti-Semitism manifested in Viseu only on two occasions each year—at Christmas and at Easter. The Catholic church was located in the center of town, and the priests there were always anti-Semitic. After midnight mass on Christmas Eve, it was not safe for a Jew to be on the street, because when the kids came out of church, they were always throwing snowballs or even stones. The trouble would begin with the Catholic boys, and the Jewish boys were subjected to beatings.

Easter was even worse. After the sermon, Jews could not be seen on the street for a day or two because they would be beaten or have stones thrown at them. Eventually, we would get hold of the boys who had thrown the stones, and we would get even. It was an ongoing conflict. Apart from those fights between kids, however, the relationship between Jews and non-Jews was a fairly good one. Adults never had fights or arguments, other than once in a while among drunkards in a bar.

In the late 1930s, however, Germans from Germany came to the area to recruit the local Volksdeutsch for various German organizations, including the SS. Then the latent anti-Semitism came out into the open.

The Coming Darkness

As Germany grew more powerful in the 1930s, its influence over
Romania, Hungary, and other Eastern European countries became
more pronounced. Romania's anti-Semitic forces were bolstered by
Hitler's rise to power in 1933, and their influence was felt within the
Romanian national government. The government of Romania was
called democratic, but it wasn't. In the 1930s, the principal political
parties were the National Peasants Party, headed by Julius Maniu, and
the Liberal Party, run by Constantin Bratianu. Maniu was an anti-
Semite, Bratianu was not. Maniu was the prime minister from 1928
until his resignation in 1931. In 1930, King Carol II returned from
exile and established a royal dictatorship for the next ten years.

Under King Carol, anti-Semitism would be the official national policy, but its severity varied from one region of the country to another.
Romania continued to be divided into what amounted to fiefdoms.
Each so-called state or substate had its own story. In Bukovina, the area
to the east and north of us on the other side of the Carpathians, anti-
Semitism was rampant. The largest city in Bukovina, Cernowitz, was
an intellectual center known as a second Budapest or Paris. But the officials there were less corrupt than elsewhere, so they were not as sus-
ceptible to bribes. In Marmaros, where there was far more corruption,
there was also less anti-Semitism. You could easily bribe officials and
buy them out of their harassment of Jews.

Three days after Christmas in 1937, King Carol installed the nation's first avowedly anti-Semitic government. There was a co-pre-
miership of Octavian Goga, a nationally renowned poet, and A. C.

Cuza, a veteran Jew-baiter. The new government, which became more Nazi than the Germans, moved quickly to strip more than half of the nation's Jews of their citizenship. Jewish businesses were seized and Jews were deprived of jobs and education. This regime lasted little more than a month, but a pattern was set in Romania that in the next few years would virtually destroy the third-largest Jewish population in Europe.

In the late 1930s, as the Second World War approached, numerous towns in Romania had pogroms. Many people were killed. In contrast, however, there were portions of the country where Jews were able to buy off government officials and the pogroms. The reason why Romania had no concentration camps in World War II was that, from the king on down, all the officials were corrupt. It was only a question of price. At the same time, the Jews of Romania had a very strong sense of communal responsibility.

The Jews in Bucharest and other large cities were irreligious. They also were the wealthier ones, and they protected other Jews from the anti-Semitic laws. For instance, there was a law that Jews must keep their stores open on Sabbath. To the irreligious Jews, this did not make any difference. Nevertheless, they went out on strike. "If you are going to make the Jews in small towns keep their stores open," they said, "we will close our stores entirely."

The stores were forced to be open on Sabbath for only a few months. The government then gave up. Jews were influential because they were educated, they were cultured, and they bribed politicians. Such bribery, called "bakshish," was practiced extensively in that part of the world for a long time. It was not viewed as a crime, the way it would have been in the United States. It was just part of the cost of doing business.

Bribery was what determined the extent of the pogroms against the Jews. I vividly remember one event. Every town had a market day once a week. In each town it was held on a different day. Peddlers with their horses and wagons came to sell pots and pans, shoes, foodstuff, and whatever they felt they could make money on. The market days were part of our way of life. On one of those days in the late 1930s, members of the Iron Guards, a Romanian anti-Semitic movement, came to our town and tried to rouse the local peasants. "The

Jews are controlling your economy," the Iron Guards said. "The Jews are controlling your way of life. Let's rise up. Let's kill them." But it did not happen. Our town never had a pogrom. Yet many other places in Romania did, especially in the villages.

In a pogrom people went from house to house, door to door, with a knife and killed Jews. It was as simple as that. Someone went into a house, pulled out the occupants, and killed them. They didn't run anybody out of town. They killed them.

Why were some towns exempted from this? Each town had a gendarme who ruled with a lot of authority. People listened to him. A town might have two or three of these gendarmes. Some were reasonably good people. They were not all anti-Semitic. Neither was the individual Romanian an anti-Semite. The problem came only when they were stirred up by the haters and self-serving politicians.

The gendarmes could be bribed—and every town had its fixer, called a "shtadlan." The Jews knew it was necessary to deal with the fixers in order to do business with gendarmes or other officials. My father, however, dealt directly with our town's gendarme rather than the local fixer.

The Romanians in our area were fairly isolated on their small farms. It was difficult, therefore, to arouse them. But in villages in other parts of the country, where two or three hundred Romanians lived close together, peasants sometimes could be aroused by buying them drinks. They were poor people, and sometimes it was only a question of the hater's ability to convince them to go and carry out a bloody pogrom. The persuaders just bought them drinks, which were very, very cheap.

In 1938, when war clouds were beginning to form, people started to think, "What do we do?" I remember many meetings in our house with my father and his friends. They went back and forth: "Should we emigrate, should we not emigrate?" The most talked about destination was Argentina. Nobody could go to the United States because of its quota system, even though at that time my father had four brothers living in the states, one of them very wealthy.

A lot of discussions took place. There was an organization called

Jewish Colonization in Argentina. Baron von Hirsch, a colleague of the Rothschilds, had created a fund for Jews to leave, mainly from Romania, for Argentina. That is what many Jews from our area had done before, during, and shortly after the First World War. Today thousands of their descendants live in Argentina and Uruguay. Everyone wanted to go to the United States, but South America was the only place to which people could easily emigrate between 1919 and the early 1940s.

There also was talk about the possibility of going to Palestine. Going there, however, posed several major problems. First, you had to have a certificate from the British, who allowed only a small number of people in. Then, the way of life and the standard of living in Palestine were very tough. One needed considerable money just to get to Palestine; once there, more money was needed to buy land or to establish a business. It was difficult and expensive to buy land. The Arabs were discouraged from selling land to Jews, and the restrictions of the British Mandate made it even more difficult. Having friends there helped one get started. But few of those who wished to emigrate had the skills or professional training needed in Palestine.

Another problem was that the way of life in our area of Romania was Hasidic, religious. In Palestine it was mostly irreligious. Most of the new immigrants were anti-religious, atheists. There were some exceptions—there was a small religious Zionist movement—but very few. So, for a family to abandon their way of life and move to Palestine was difficult. To go there, you really had to be a single person and you had to go as a pioneer, building kibbutzim and roads. There were a lot of people who did go to Palestine, but they were sixteen, seventeen, and eighteen years old; not many were older people.

There were some German Jews who went to Palestine who were very rich. They could buy whatever they needed. But even then it was difficult because of the standard of living and the way of life there. Few Romanian Jews emigrated to Palestine, although the discussions about going there went on constantly in the 1930s. The only practical possibility was Argentina.

In the late 1930s it became increasingly difficult to do business in Romania because of the growing violence of the Romanian Iron Guards and their anti-Jewish campaign. Their calls for the exclusion of Jews from all facets of Romanian life were gradually adopted by all political parties and government coalitions.

It was very difficult to travel from town to town. My father still had to go to the bigger cities to buy the merchandise he sold in his store. With each passing day in the last years before the war, more and more Jews were beaten and thrown from trains. Our whole way of life was being challenged; that was the reason behind those discussions of my father and his friends about emigration. But nothing materialized; emigration for our large family was not feasible. By 1940 there were eight children in our family.

On March 13, 1938, with the Anschluss, Austria was incorporated into the Reich and the German border expanded to Hungary. In March of 1939, as a result of Neville Chamberlain's appeasement at Munich, Hitler marched into the Sudetenland of Czechoslovakia. The Czech government collapsed. The Germans then moved into Prague. Slovakia, under Father Tiso, a Catholic priest, was declared by Hitler to be an independent state.

As talk of war increased, the children of Viseu began to be involved. I was twelve. We listened to the radio from time to time—by then there were a few radios in town. We knew what was going on. The anti-Semitism increased, but only from the Germans. The ordinary Romanians in and around our town were still very civil and not anti-Semitic.

After the Sudetenland was occupied by the Germans, the part of Marmaros north of the Tisa River, which had been part of Czechoslovakia, was given by Hitler to Hungary. That was where my mother's hometown was. For the next year and a half she was unable to cross the new border and see her father in Vilchovitz.

On August 30, 1940, the Germans decreed that northern Transylvania, including Marmaros south of the Tisa, was "returned" from Romania to Hungary. The area affected by the decree contained 130,000 Jews, including my family. In October, the German army moved into Romania. Hungary, of which we were now a part, joined the Axis Powers, thereby increasing its military cooperation with Germany.

Hungarian control of Marmaros, both north and south of the Tisa, meant that our area was once again united with no borders. We could again visit my grandfather. But little else about being added to Hungary was good. Hungary had been waiting for twenty years to recover its former territory. Between the two World Wars, Romania and Hungary were at a sword's edge because at the end of the first war Hungary lost all of Transylvania to Romania. Portions of Hungary were also used to create the new nations of Czechoslovakia and Yugoslavia. The result was that Hungary became small when measured against the once vast Austro-Hungarian Empire. One of the consequences was that many bureaucrats had to be recalled to Hungary. They could not stay; they no longer had jobs. The departing Hungarians had said, "We'll be back, we'll be back—eventually." Now they returned, as our judges, postal officials, mayors, and police.

In 1935 Hitler had enacted his Nuremberg Laws, taking away virtually all rights from Jews in Germany. After that Hungary put into effect its own set of racial laws. One set of laws was for Hungarian Jews and the other was for Jews who came under Hungarian control in the occupied areas of Czechoslovakia and Romania. The native Hungarian Jews were treated substantially better. For example, Jews were drafted into the Hungarian army until well into the war. But the so-called inherited Jews in the occupied countries were treated much worse.

The difference was noticed quickly in our region. There had been relatively little anti-Semitism in Marmaros under the old Austro-Hungarian Empire or under the corrupt Romanian government. It is true that the local priests aroused their congregations, telling them that the Jews killed Jesus. And as Germany became more powerful, there were more and more German tourists in our scenic area in the late 1930s, and local Germans began falling under the influence of anti-Semitic German organizations and even volunteering to go to Germany to serve in the SS. But the situation became much worse after August 1940 when Hungarian officials returned with a national policy of anti-Semitism. I was almost fourteen at the time.

I especially remember one incident that happened on Easter Sunday. A Hungarian soldier, riding what looked to me to be a giant horse (the Hungarian hussars were great riders with beautiful horses), told me that I "killed Jesus." I responded that I had not. "Yes," he said, "you did it," and he told his horse to jump on me. Fortunately, I was able to get away. The soldier had just come out of church.

In 1941, my father arranged for me to attend the yeshiva in Sekelhid. The town was known as the goose capital of the world. The people there raised geese by the hundreds of thousands for their feathers, their fat, and their livers. Pâté was exported to France and all over the world. In the town itself there were only 120 Jews, but they had a famous rabbi, Yehuda Rosner, and a famous yeshiva that I attended for a year.

The stores in Sekelhid were filled with merchandise. So I used to buy as much as I could and send it home to my parents. The train left Sekelhid by ten o'clock each morning and arrived in Viseu each evening. I shipped home goose meat.

Before World War II the better students left their hometowns and attended yeshivas in other places. As students in 1941, we were still permitted by the Hungarian government to travel. But going to the yeshiva in Sekelhid was not that simple. Boys over thirteen or fourteen had to belong to paramilitary brigades. But Jewish boys were not allowed to practice with arms; we performed manual labor. Once a week we had to take part, doing pointless work.

We had to bring stones from the nearby river, for example, and dig holes in which to put them. This was done under the direction of the Hungarian military. Non-Jewish teenagers were given military training, but Jews were not. Instead, Jews from age eighteen to forty-five were drafted into labor battalions called "Munka Solgalot." Jewish boys under eighteen had to attend what was called a leventa, and for our work each week we would receive an identification card that had to be stamped. The police or soldiers would stop you on the street many, many times and demand that you show your identification. They stopped everybody. You could not go on the street for half an hour without being stopped—especially males of possible draft age.

If you were younger, you were stopped for the purpose of harassment, and often they would beat you. The Hungarian soldiers were very anti-Semitic. From time to time one also encountered border police, a division of the national police. The national police wore large, black derby hats with feathers. The border police wore typical military hats but also with feathers. When you saw them, you ran away because you knew that they would beat you just for the sake of beating you.

In the course of weekly make-work, we often had to drag military wagons carrying ammunition in the rain and snow. Sekelhid was hilly, and we had to pull those wagons up those hills while the soldiers were beating us with guns and whips. Then, if you didn't have your ID stamped, you risked another beating. When you traveled, you always had to be sure you had your ID. Despite all this, I was able to send items home, and both my father and mother came to visit me on separate occasions.

On June 22, 1941, Germany attacked the Soviet Union from the Baltic to the Black Sea. Joining in the attack were both Hungarian and Romanian forces. On June 27, the Jews in what had been Czech Marmaros were ordered by the Hungarian government to prove that their families had uninterrupted residency for the previous ninety years, that is, from the year 1851, and that their ancestors had been listed among the taxpayers. In *Atlas of the Holocaust,* historian Martin Gilbert describes what happened next:

> [M]any of the Jews of Marmaros—and it seems they were the majority—did not react to the citizenship-decree, as to a real and present danger. With their simple mode of thinking, they could not conceive of the satanic scheme which was being woven around this decree. They knew, and the whole world knew, that not only they, but also their parents and ancestors were born and died in this land (and of course were heavily taxed). These Jews, therefore, did not make the effort to produce the necessary documents for citizenship. The struggle for a loaf of bread, literally speaking, prevented them from thinking along those lines; many of them simply did not have the necessary sum of money needed to arrange for the documents.

In the summer and fall of 1941, tens of thousands of Jews were uprooted from their ancestral towns north of the Tisa River and exiled to Galicia in Poland, where they were subsequently murdered by the Hungarians or died from starvation. It was the beginning of the Holocaust in our part of the world.

It is all burned into my memory. My aunt and her parents were among those Jews killed by the Hungarians. Most of the victims were Jews of Polish origin, others Russian or Ukrainian. It happened in all the towns and villages in the newly occupied part of Hungary, large and small. Many families were completely wiped out.

One of my aunts and her parents had been born in Vilchovitz, my mother's town, but her grandparents had been born in Ukraine. She was deported. In Viseu, south of the Tisa, there were very few people whose families originally had come from Poland, but the Hungarians picked up those few and transported them across the border back to Poland.

The Hungarians had returned en masse to our town in September of 1940. They previously had decided who was going to be the mayor, the judge, and the police chief for each town in the area. There was only about a week's time in which the Romanian officials left and the Hungarians arrived. The Hungarians put their bureaucratic system into effect almost overnight.

A few of the Germans in town started to celebrate this takeover by their allies. All public positions were immediately filled. The Hungarians brought in a judge who was the most anti-Semitic one they could find. He was from the Czech side, and he knew exactly what he was expected to do. The Hungarians were more meticulous in their organization than the Romanians, who were more "seat-of-the-pants" types. The Hungarians knew that the local method of doing business had not been according to the book. Now, under the Hungarians, any violation of the law, whether it was real law or a perceived one, was subject to a jail sentence. Within a few days of the Hungarian takeover, my father was taken to jail for some infringement of some law. The Romanians could always be bought—it was just a question of cost. But the Hungarians could not.

It was the Hungarians' practice—and that of the Germans, too—to come to a town and arrest the leaders, the rich people. Often they were industrialists or other business people. Sometimes they would be shot in order to induce fear in the Jewish population. The new judge in our town did not kill anyone, but he arrested key people. My father was in custody for about a week and there was a trial—I don't remember the charges. He must have paid a fine because he was let out.

There were barracks in our town for Hungarian soldiers. The Hungarians also began drafting Jews into labor battalions where they were used as human minesweepers. They were forced to walk in front of the Hungarian and German troops. If mines were encountered, the Jews were killed. The Jews in the labor service were required to wear civilian clothes with a military cap and a yellow armband. They were given no weapons. Many, many thousands were killed. The members of these battalions ranged from eighteen to forty-five years in age.

Within a few days after the Hungarians arrived in Viseu, they started implementing anti-Semitic laws. Stores must be open on Sabbath. Jews could not travel. They could not buy land—they could still own it, but not buy it. No contract with Jews was valid. All Jews in the occupied lands were required to produce documentation showing that they were natives—not an easy thing to prove, since many Jews, as well as gentiles, did not register their children at birth in order to avoid having them drafted into the army when they came of age. Others had never applied for citizenship though their families had lived in the area for a hundred years or more.

And there were the labor battalions. Among those drafted was my father, who was selected in 1941 at the age of forty-three. At the time he was probably one of the oldest taken. He was transported by bus many hours away to a town called Bistrita. The members of the battalions thought that they were going to be shipped north to the former Czech territory. My father made a decision that he would pay any amount of money to get out because, by that time, he had eight children and felt he had to keep his business going.

My father looked around for a fixer, someone who had access to a person who was in charge of the military. Finally there was someone my father was told he might approach. The man said, "I can't guarantee anything. These guys are tough." But he added that he was willing to take a chance, and my father said, "What have I got to lose?" So my father took a big chunk of money—I don't remember how much—and said, "Here it is. I'm putting this down. If it works, it works. If it doesn't, it doesn't."

That was on a Sunday. On Monday morning he was expected to march out with the labor battalion. So Sunday night he turned over the money. He did not know what was going to happen to it—

whether it would be paid or whether he would be put in jail. Monday morning there was a roll call. There were hundreds, maybe thousands, of men there, and they were given orders to move out. Anyone whose name was called had to go. Anyone whose name was not called was to go home. Everybody's name was called—except my father's. So he came home. He was the only one. He was never drafted again.

Most of those men later suffered greatly. They were kept for a long time. In fact, few ever returned home. They were generally used in front of the infantry and were killed.

After the deportation and murder of Jews from Marmaros in the summer and fall of 1941, Hungarian policy changed for a while in 1942. Part of it was due to world pressure. Another reason was, perhaps, that Admiral Horthy, the regent, had a son who was married to a Jewish woman, and she may have had some influence. Also, for a while, there was a prime minister appointed by Horthy, M. Kallay, who was more lenient. But this did not last for long. Horthy's son was soon killed by the Germans in a plane crash.

An additional reason for the period of leniency was that many of the Hungarian leaders were very pragmatic. They always were concerned about hedging their bet. They said, "Wait a minute. We'll do some good things so if the war does not go our way, we will have some alibis about what happened." Because of the bet-hedging, Horthy was not one of the war criminals executed at the war's end. In October of 1944 he issued a public statement about the Jewish question, "the solution of which the Gestapo had dealt with in the way that . . . was against the principles of humanity." But by then the Soviets had overrun half of Hungary. He was arrested by the Germans, survived, and subsequently sought to justify himself to the Allied authorities. But the Holocaust of the Hungarian Jews had already occurred. Horthy had been an ally of Hitler from day one, even before Italy and Japan.

Once the Hungarians had taken over our area, the economy started to deteriorate rapidly because the people were not permitted to conduct commerce the way they previously had. The local Germans became very anti-Semitic. There was a steady flow of agitators from the Reich who recruited the local German youth into the Bund, which became very active.

It was difficult to do business with the Germans. We also were unable to engage in the types of so-called extracurricular business that had been important. We could not buy lumber, for example. Other transactions became too risky. You also couldn't travel. The fruit orchard business was gone. You couldn't buy the loads of cabbage. It was dangerous to travel on trains. There were all sorts of attacks on Jews. My father and other businessmen couldn't travel to the big cities to buy supplies to sell. There were shortages and rationing.

The rationing resulted in a black market, because what you were able to get under the rationing was not sufficient to live on. And the black market economy became dangerous because the police were engaged in constant surveillance and were very rigid. If caught, you could not buy yourself out. So business became very difficult for everybody. I was now a teenager, and as the war went on, my mother and I were the ones who traveled a lot. It was less dangerous for my mother than it was for my father. It was difficult, however, because she had to leave her children at home.

In 1940 and 1941, the Romanian stores and warehouses had been stuffed with merchandise, but Hungary had shortages. They could not, for example, obtain any items from the Far East. Coffee, pepper, spices, and other condiments were in great shortage. When the Hungarians occupied Marmaros, they couldn't believe that the stores still had cinnamon, black pepper, and coffee. They bought all the supplies they could lay their hands on. It took about eight months before the stores were emptied. Then our area, like Hungary, experienced severe shortages. Moreover, people stopped paying my father for their goods. There was a new currency now, and customers ceased paying on old accounts.

All the while, Hungarian soldiers kept passing through town, going to and from Poland, Ukraine, and the eastern front. There also were occasional German and Italian troops. The Italians, some of whom were stationed in our town for a while, were decent people. We had fun with them. They gave us food. We could talk with them a little because Romanian and Italian are somewhat similar languages.

What remained of the economy was still largely conducted and controlled by Jews. But now they could not own stores by themselves. They had to have a non-Jewish partner. And the stores had to remain open on all Jewish holidays. The non-Jewish partners usually were unable to run the businesses properly, so the whole economy fell apart. At first my father had a partner but, after a while, the partner said he wanted to own the store by himself. My father was fed up. He closed the store and we had nothing. This was in late 1943.

In 1943 we knew that the war was getting closer to us, that the Russians were advancing. In fact, when we eventually left Viseu, the Russians were only about a hundred kilometers away. Through German-language Hungarian newspapers and the BBC, we also knew that the Allies were advancing in North Africa and Italy. We always felt we were safe. We experienced hardships, but we were sure they would come to an end with the Russians moving closer. Soon the suffering would be over. Just let the Russians keep coming!

People talked constantly about the war and how it would end. They went to synagogue. What did they do afterwards? They didn't have to hurry anywhere. They had no place to go, so they just sat and talked and speculated about the war. Everyone was an armchair general. We were always confident that we knew what should be done, based on the information we had.

There was increasing poverty in the area. Because of the lack of food, we sometimes ground dried peas into flour to make bread. It was palatable enough, but the odor was terrible.

Somehow my mother always managed to have food in our house. The Sabbath and the holidays virtually kept the Jewish people alive. For Sabbath we had the Friday night meal. For it you made white bread, called challah. Officially, you were not allowed by the government to have it. So if you did, you obviously had obtained it on the black market. Because of this, when we sat down to the meal, my mother did something rare—she locked the door in case somebody came by unexpectedly. If anyone came to the door, we hid the bread right away but let them in because no one ever kept their door locked.

Things went on in a state of gradual deterioration until 1944. Then we began to hear that terrible events were happening. We had not known about the concentration camps. Some people from the work brigades came home from Poland and Ukraine and spoke of atrocities they had seen, but we simply did not believe what they told us about killings and mass graves. We heard them, but we never believed them.

Elie Wiesel, who lived in nearby Sighet, said after the war: "The Jews of Sighet didn't know what awaited them, until the last minute . . . a year after the Warsaw Ghetto uprising, we still did not know a thing concerning the Nazi plan to exterminate European Jewry." There were no newspapers to report anything about mass killings, and no radio programs. Everything was censored. But everyone's nerves grew strained, and no one knew what the next day would hold. We heard stories about the Russians attacking on the eastern front, but the propaganda was very heavily German. Occasionally someone would hear something on the BBC, and sometimes there were disturbing rumors. During those early months of 1944, our whole way of life, our mental outlook and our behavior, changed dramatically. The atmosphere was very oppressive and very depressing.

We heard that my aunt had been taken from her town in Czech Marmaros in 1941 and transported to Poland. It was only after the war, however, that we found out that she had been murdered together with her parents. Rumors came back, but nobody was sure. The deported Jews had been dead for a long time, but Hungarian soldiers and others came back to our town with messages that people were still alive. The soldiers kept the Jews' hopes up so that they could be milked for more bribe money.

We continued to hear of the killings of individual Jews in Poland, Ukraine, and Russia, but we never heard anything about concentration camps. We heard nothing of them—until we came to Auschwitz.

My father's youngest brother, Buroch, was drafted into a Hungarian work brigade in 1942. He had six children and was considered to be one of the richer men in Viseu. He owned a large store in the center of town and did a lot to help people in need without letting them know where the help came from.

He was sent to the Soviet front in Ukraine. During the winter of 1943 many of the men in his brigade contracted typhus. In March of that year, the Germans put as many as eight hundred of them into a hospital in the town of Dorshetz and set it on fire. Those who tried to escape were machine-gunned to death. Nobody survived. Everyone inside the building was burned to death. We found out about it only after the war in 1946. The story of what happened came from a Jew who was one of the few healthy ones in the area at the time and was not placed in the hospital.

A child of Buroch was born after he was killed. His wife did not know he was dead. But then neither she nor their children survived. My aunt and her six children would soon be murdered at Auschwitz.

As 1944 began, economic conditions deteriorated even further. There was a lack of food, supplies, money, and commerce. The last time I traveled for my mother was in March of 1944 when I went north of the Tisa River to my grandfather's village. In the rich farm-ing area around Tecs, I was able to find eggs, flour, and other staples, which I loaded into a suitcase to bring home.

Returning home, I had to stop at a station to change trains. Soldiers came and asked me what I was doing. "What do you have in that suit-case?" they asked. They opened it and saw that everything I was car-rying was contraband. They beat me and took me to the nearest police station.

This happened on the day before Purim. Jews were on their way to the synagogue. I was confined all night, but in the morning I was re-leased. My mother and father were not aware of what had happened to me. There were no phones, so it was impossible to communicate. I arrived home on a Thursday, and it was the last time I traveled until I was deported that May. It was on that day in March of 1944 that the German troops moved into Hungary. They occupied Budapest and took over the government. Adolf Eichmann was prepared for his ac-tivities in both Hungary and the occupied territories.

Organized life in our town fell apart. Our rabbi was arrested and thrown into jail. He had attempted to help people by providing birth certificates for those who did not have one. Due to his arrest and the harassment of the other town leaders, community organizations ceased functioning. I learned recently of our rabbi's final days from Professor Michael Klein. He was with Rabbi Hager in Auschwitz. After Rabbi Hager's arrest in the summer of 1943, he was sent to the area's most infamous jail in Kistarcsa near Budapest. There he languished until the summer of 1944, at which time he was sent to Auschwitz. In January 1945 when Auschwitz was evacuated ahead of advancing Russian troops, he and thousands of others were transported in open rail cars westward. They traveled this way in the dead of winter for approximately twelve days. Upon arrival in a town near Brno, Czechoslovakia, on January 27, 1945, the bodies in the rail cars were encrusted with ice and had to be separated with axes. Rabbi Hager and twenty-six others in his rail car were found dead. Oskar Schindler's factory work camp was there in town and he personally supervised the burial in a mass grave there.

The anti-Semitism of the local Germans then became atrocious. You could not walk on the street without taking great risks. We were more fortunate than the other Jews in the area because we still had some dialogue with our town's Germans. And we were not docile. I mean we kids. If we caught a German kid who was causing trouble, we would beat him up. We were aggressive.

There was one incident I remember late in 1943. One of the local Germans, who had volunteered for the SS, came home on furlough and came into our store. Give me this, he said, and give me that. I said, "All right. Pay me."

"We don't pay anything," he replied. "I'm a German, I'm an SS."

When he refused to pay for what he had received, my father gave him a licking. So the German went to court and accused my father, who was fined.

When the Germans moved into Hungary in March of 1944, they already had their plan for what to do with the Jews. Their actions against Jews were to coincide with Jewish holidays. Much of the killing that they had carried out in Poland, Ukraine, and Russia had coincided with major Jewish holidays—Rosh Hashanah, Yom Kippur, and the others. Now, in Hungary, the Germans planned to begin their annihilation of the Jews by shipping them to death camps on the day after Passover. The Germans knew the Jews would be at home on that holiday. We would all be together. The Germans would not have to seek us out.

In March the Germans came to each major city. The Hungarians were already in place. The Hungarian border police did the dirty work. The Germans gave the orders to start preparing lists of all the

Jews in every town. Then they did something they had learned was effective from their experience in Poland, Lithuania, and other countries. They created a Judenrat, a council of appointed Jewish leaders.

Before Passover, the Germans called the Judenrat in and told them that the front lines were changing rapidly and that the Russians were coming very close. For two reasons, the Germans said, the Jews had to be taken away and moved into central Hungary. Reason One was that the Germans did not want anyone to get hurt, and it would be safer there. Reason Two was that the Germans needed a workforce deeper in Hungary, where the land was very fertile. "A lot of grain grows there," they said, "and we need you to help. You will be together with your families."

"So," the Germans told the Jewish leaders, "we need to have a list of every Jew in town and the list has to be turned over on Passover Eve and nobody is going to have Passover holiday unless we have this list." That order was given in March, just a couple of weeks before Passover.

In our town we did not know at first exactly what was happening, but we knew that the German military had come in. As we gradually learned more about their plan to move people away, my father and I started to think: "Wait a minute. This doesn't make sense. Maybe we should run away to hide. The area is all mountainous and we know it as well as anybody, and the soldiers don't know it."

First my father talked to members of a German family, people close to us, and asked them to hide us because we did not believe the authorities were giving us truthful information. So we packed up and moved out to the family's place and were hidden in a barn. We were there two days at most. We wondered how we could survive and thought that maybe the family might turn us in.

We did not know about the concentration camps. We did not know about the gas chambers, the crematoria, about Auschwitz. All we knew was that the people were to be moved away and that the Russians were not far from us. For weeks the Germans had been retreating from the southern part of Ukraine and Poland into our town. Many soldiers had come back looking defeated. They were not the type of soldiers that we had seen before in the pictures of the Germans. Now they looked bedraggled and haggard.

They were retreating, as were the Italians. We thus concluded that the Russians were very close. In fact, by April 15, we were later to learn, the Russians were just across the mountains in Bukovina, having liberated the city of Cernowitz. The mountains between us were high, more than seven thousand feet, but the Russians were on the other side.

My father decided that hiding in that barn was not going to work. How would we get food for our family? I think he also became suspicious of the German family who owned the barn because of something they said. Something must have aroused his suspicions. He decided that we should go back to town.

So we went back to town. The Judenrat prepared a list of all the Jews. I don't know how lists for the outlying villages were compiled, but I assume in a similar manner. Orders were given and all the Jews from outlying villages were herded into ghettos. One was in our town. The next was in Sighet. These were the pick-up points through which the trains ran.

All of those people could have run away, could have hidden. There were not enough Hungarian or German soldiers in the vicinity to stop them. In fact, in our town there were only two German officers, and they were responsible for the whole area. Even the Hungarian gendarmes were not sufficient in numbers to round up all the people if they wanted to run away. No way.

Many, if not most, of the Jews came from villages that were in rugged terrain. They knew the countryside; they could have hidden as long as they wanted and they didn't need much to live on. They could have gone and escaped the horror to come.

The day after Passover the Germans created a ghetto in the center of our town. Every Jew from our town and the outlying area had to go there. They herded in as many people as they could. We were fortunate because my Uncle Buroch's big house is where we were sent, along with my two aunts who lived in the nearby towns of Moisei and Borsa. Our four families were in that house. We had been moved there from our own homes with only what we could carry. No more.

Day by day people were brought from the outlying villages to the ghetto. Within a week the villages had been emptied.

The Germans had it all planned. They employed disinformation and deception. There was a doctor from our town, for example, who the Germans said was going to take care of the people in one of the villages, and nothing would happen to him. But when the last train from our town carried away his family, it stopped in that village and picked him up too. To pacify the people and to make them think everything was going to be all right, the Germans had left him in the village until he had served their purpose.

The people from outlying villages came with their wagons and anything they could carry. I don't know how they were able to get food. We were fortunate because we were able to sneak out of the ghetto and get some food. You were supposed to have a permit to leave, but there was no wire fence, just guards, and we knew how to sneak out. We went to our house and got whatever we could.

Before my father left our house, which was outside the ghetto, he buried two boxes under a chicken coop and a storage room. They contained some valuables, some fancy linen bedspreads and my mother's kerchief and apron—things of that nature. Whatever money we had we took along with us. It was not buried but was hidden in the attic of my uncle's house in the ghetto.

We were in that house only three or four weeks. During that time, at the Germans' insistence the Hungarians promulgated many new laws. Among them was that men's beards were to be cut off and women had to have short hair. Every day there were new rules and regulations. All this was disseminated to us by the Judenrat. They were doing the bidding of the Germans. The Germans merely sat and gave the orders.

I was seventeen years old. A few teenage friends of mine and I decided one day, "To hell with it. We're not going to be taken any place. We're going away to the country, away to the woods." Summer was coming. It was already the beginning of May. It was still cold, but there was no more snow. We decided to run away, to leave the ghetto. It would take only a few minutes to get to the woods. One boy told his father of our plans. I did not tell mine. The boy's father informed a member of the Judenrat who became very concerned. No, he said, we couldn't do that.

When my father learned of this concern, he said we should hear what the old man had to say about our idea. People in our town were always soliciting and giving advice. They might not do what they were advised, but they listened.

So the other boy and I went with our fathers to hear what the Judenrat had to say. You can't run away, they said. You know you would be jeopardizing the others. You would be punished. Furthermore, they added, there was nothing to worry about. Everything was under control.

At that time the first trainload of Jews had already left our town, heading for Auschwitz.

My paternal grandmother, Fradel Traubkatz Tessler, who gave me two pieces of candy for knowing my school lessons. This photo probably was taken when my Uncle Peter visited Viseu in 1926. After I came to America, he gave me a copy.

My mother
and father
when they
were engaged
in 1925.

My mother (center) in her hometown of Vilchovitz in Czechoslovakia.
With her are her two sisters. Udel Oestereicher (left) perished with her
husband and their three children in Auschwitz. Ginendel Grinwald
was also murdered there with her six children. Her husband, Berl, survived and lives in Monsey, New York. This photograph was taken in
1922 or 1923, when my mother was seventeen or eighteen years old.

Grave No. 2 at Bergen-Belsen, which contains the remains of five thousand inmates. The grave was closed April 23, 1945, eight days after the death camp was liberated by the British army. My wife's sister, Rose Hoffmann Davies, and Rose's husband, Marvin Davies, visited in the fall of 1945. Another of my wife's sisters, Blanka, who had been a prisoner at Bergen-Belsen along with Edith and Rose, died from typhus a week before the liberation and is buried in this grave. She was one of the twenty-three thousand inmates at the camp who died from the effects of starvation and disease in the days immediately before and after liberation.

The Train Turned North
to Auschwitz

When the process of ghettoization began in mid-April 1944 in the Hungarian territories, the areas to be closed were declared areas of military operations. In Transylvania, which included Romanian Marmaros, the Jews were forced into seven ghettos containing a total of 97,000 people.

The deportations to Auschwitz began on May 15, 1944, and by May 24 between 8,000 and 14,000 Jews were being sent out of the Hungarian territories every day, for a total of 106,000 people in a ten-day period. All the squads working in the gas chambers and the "canada" warehouses in Auschwitz were reinforced, and the crematoria were kept working twenty-four hours a day.

Because there was a demand for railway cars from the German army retreating along the Russian front, Adolf Eichmann, in carrying out the mass executions, was forced to make do with four trains a day, instead of the six he had requested through the offices of the Hungarian government. But he crammed eighty to one hundred people into each cattle car with a normal capacity of forty. The trains traveled via Ruthenia and Galicia, the latter being part of Poland. As far as the border station of Czap, Hungarian police were responsible for guarding the transports. At Czap they were turned over to SS guards, who opened the doors primarily to remove the bodies of those who had died along the way.

Every two days the Hungarian gendarmes took away another trainload of people. From Viseu they went in boxcars, about ninety persons to a car, and they had with them only what they could carry. They were just taken away.

After we learned that the first group had been taken, we wanted, more than ever, to run away. But the town elders, the Judenrat, continued to insist that we shouldn't worry because everything was "under control." They said that we were going to go near Mezokaszomy, a town deep in Hungary. One of the elders showed us a postcard that had been received by the parents of a boy named Kestner, a neighbor of ours who was in a labor battalion. It said that he had seen a trainload of people from our area who had been brought to Mezokaszomy in the heart of Hungary's wheat-growing country. Everything, the boy said, was all right. It was, of course, the Germans who actually wrote that card. They had the names of people who were in certain areas, like that boy, and they had the names and addresses of their relatives back home. It was typical of the Germans. They did that all over Hungary. They did the same in Poland and all over the areas from which they herded Jews into ghettos or moved them to concentration camps.

In Viseu we were told that the card was confirmation of what the elders had been telling us. But, as we would soon find out, it was not true. We were taken away on the third transport. It was Sunday, May 21, 1944.

Everybody was taken—my father, my mother, my brothers, sisters, aunts, uncles, cousins, and me—some ninety people in a boxcar. Ironically, the member of the Judenrat who had shown us the postcard was taken to Auschwitz on the fourth transport. He tried to kill himself when he found out what was happening. He took cyanide but was saved and carried to Auschwitz on a stretcher. He realized that he could have saved us by letting us run away.

We left on that Sunday on a train that went northwest to Sighet. We were headed toward Hungary. From the border town of Czap one set of tracks ran west to Hungary. Other tracks led north to Poland. At Czap, the train turned north to go to Poland instead of west to Hungary. My father told us we were definitely not headed for Mezokaszomy. He knew his geography. The train was going somewhere else. "We have big problems," my father said. We realized we had been lied to, but there was nothing we could do.

At Czap, not only had the train turned north, but something else happened. The guards were changed. The Hungarians were replaced by the SS. The locomotive was different. It was from the German railroads, not the Hungarian lines.

The path the train took from Viseu to Auschwitz, 1944.

Then, all of a sudden, there was screaming—all sorts of screaming—"Los, los, los," "Let's go, move, move, move." Those doing the
shouting were the SS. They were ethnic Germans from Romania,
Hungary, and Yugoslavia, wherever Germans lived. There also were
Ukrainians and Lithuanians who volunteered for those brigades because of their ingrained anti-Semitism. We had been let out of the
boxcars for a few minutes and were being ordered back. They did not
have a chance to beat us because we moved quickly.

We traveled north into Poland and, by that time, the stench was terrible. We kept emptying the buckets that were all we had for our san-
itary needs. We still had some of the food my mother packed for us.
She also had some pots and pans with her that she intended to use for
cooking in Mezokaszomy. They were special pots and pans for
preparing all kinds of foods.

On Wednesday, May 24, after dark, we arrived at Auschwitz. The
doors of the cattle cars were opened and there was much shouting and
screaming—"Los, los, los." I saw the guards with the dogs, and there
were many beatings.

Then there was that greeting: "Hello, Esther." It was from the
German who had lived across the street from us, a twenty-year-old
with whom I had grown up. My mother had baked cakes for the family for the year-end holiday season. He had volunteered for the SS.
Once he had come back to our hometown on furlough wearing his
uniform. He was one of the guards at Auschwitz. He was no better, no
worse than the others.

In the darkness on that Wednesday night in May we were ordered
to line up, men on one side, women on the other, and the guards began
their beatings. Then they started to march us and shouted, "You go
left, you go right." There was a German with a small baton at the head
of the line who pointed left, then right. Initially we did not know what
that meant, but eventually we found out. Left meant that you went to
a work site. Right meant to the gas chamber.

We were separated from our mother. My father, two of my brothers, and I went to one side and my mother, three sisters, and three
youngest brothers went to the other. That was the end. At that time
we didn't know that we would never see them again.

We went to one side and into a room where we were ordered to undress amidst all the screaming, the beatings, and the shouts of "Hurry, hurry" and "Don't ask questions." "Leave everything here," the Germans shouted. "You can't take anything with you except your shoes." Only my shoes and my glasses. That is all I had.

Each of us had a little prayer book. My father kept some money in his. But he had to throw it all away.

We were shaved or, more accurately, beards were slashed off with a straight razor. Then our hair was cut. In the center of our heads, a stripe was shaved. If we tried to run away, we would be recognized immediately. Then we were marched to take a shower and, when we came out of the shower room, they gave each of us a pair of striped pants, a jacket, and a cap—prisoner garb. It was then Thursday morning.

It was cold, freezing, and we were all huddling together. We had no idea of what had become of our mother, brothers, and sisters. Then, as we were huddling outside (we had not had any barracks assigned to us yet), all of a sudden I saw what had been thrown out from the side of the building where the gas chambers were. (It was all the same building. One side had the showers with water; the other had showers with Zyklon-B gas.) On the ground on the side to which the women and children had been taken were their belongings.

We were totally dazed. We could not comprehend what was going on. We were disoriented for a long time. We could not think normally. It was many, many months before we realized what had happened the night we arrived at Auschwitz.

The "canada kommandos" is what the men and women were called who took the prisoners' belongings and then separated them. They took clothes. They took money. They took everything that the women and children had been forced to discard. Everything was separated into categories and eventually shipped to Germany.

We recognized my mother's pots and pans. I remembered the very distinct ones that she had with her. We recognized them right away. We had no idea what had happened to her. All we knew was that we saw the pots and pans.

Later that same morning, we were taken to barracks and given the licorice water that the Germans called coffee. We were assigned to a board where four people could lie. It was to be our so-called bed. My father, my two brothers, and I were to be on the same board.

That was our first twenty-four hours at Auschwitz.

For many weeks, even months, after we were separated from my mother, my three sisters, and three brothers, we could not comprehend what had happened. The reason was that from the moment we were in the hands of the Germans in Czap and crossed over into Poland instead of Hungary, the Germans executed a policy that Jews were not human. We were animals, and to be treated as animals, with screaming, guard dogs, whips, and beatings. The Germans treated Jews as vermin, and vermin must be destroyed. That was manifested in every way at every moment of the day. There was never an order given without somebody being struck—men, women, and children. The Germans always had in their hands either guns or whips. They used the butts of the guns to beat us.

As soon as we arrived in Auschwitz, the dogs and the whips were there, and the screaming, "Go, go, go, go, go." It was so fast.

It was so fast that we really had no idea what was happening. It took us many, many months to comprehend what had happened those first few days in Auschwitz and, even then, I don't think we really understood. It was only much later that we understood.

When we were separated, we had no idea what happened to the people who had not come along with us, to our mother, to our brothers and sisters, to our aunts and uncles, and on and on—no idea, except for those two pots that told us that our mother had been there. It was not until much later that we figured out the reason those pots were outside the building was that our family had been taken to the gas chambers.

We knew that we had arrived on a Wednesday night and that by Thursday morning they were all gone. The pots were there. That was all.

Many prisoners never knew when their parents and their families had been murdered. It was all part of the totally evil system employed to mislead us to slaughter.

After our hair had been cut and we were shaved, we were disinfected. Those stripes on our heads were about an inch wide and were shaved from the tops of our foreheads to the backs of our heads. We were allowed to keep only our shoes and glasses. Nothing else. No prayer books. Nothing.

With every move we made, we were hit. Every inch of the way we were hit and hit and hit.

We soon learned that the day-to-day operations of the camp were in the hands of certain inmates who were mostly Jews. Those Jews who gave the orders were called block elders and capos.

In the same barracks with my father, my brothers, and me were seven young men and four older ones from our town. The older ones, except for my father, were soon taken to the other side of the building where the gas chambers were.

That first morning after our arrival, when we lay down on that board, we were all in a daze. We had no concept of what was going on. Later we were offered that so-called coffee, which was dark, brownish water, licorice water. I don't remember drinking it. About three hundred of us were in that barracks, which was run by a block elder. He had a couple of assistants who had whips in their hands and hit us at every move we made. They were very agile.

The block leader and his assistants were Jews. They had been trained to do what they did. To survive, they had to be cruel, not only vicious and crude, but as cruel as they could be. They always hit you in the stomach where it would hurt the most. One blow would cause you to scream with pain, drop to the ground, and roll over several times. Less than a week before, we had been living in our hometown. Now we were living in hell.

We were in a daze. Then suddenly there was a roll call and we were stood outside for hours. Go here! Go there! Stand here! Stand there! The roll call went on for a long time. We were told to count ourselves by numbers. Everybody counted. Then they asked who spoke German and who didn't. It was all part of their technique of dehumanizing you. That was the whole idea. The appel or roll call was done by a member of the SS. If you did not stand exactly the way he wanted, you were struck again and again.

My father, my brothers, the seven youngsters from our hometown, and I always tried to stay together. It was difficult. At about noon we were taken out of the barracks, then back into the barracks, then out again and in again for no other reason than to make life miserable and to get us used to a routine.

They brought a big kettle into the barracks. We were on those boards, the so-called beds. They gave each of us a small enamel bowl and a spoon. These were our sole possessions. They gave us some kind of soup that had probably been made with turnips and water, no meat. They gave some to my father. I was next to him. We couldn't look at the food, much less eat it. This was our first exposure there to any kind of food. And it obviously was not kosher.

My father said, "Eat." I said, "How can I eat? I can't eat this."

He said, "Please eat. You have to eat. If you don't eat, it's not going to be good." I had a bit of the turnip soup but I couldn't swallow it.

How my father suffered! How could it be that a man had three sons with him and they couldn't eat and he couldn't help them? The pain that went through him I understood many years later. He was speechless for a long, long time. His suffering at being unable to help us was to be repeated many times.

The German officer who was the camp leader was thirty years old, if that, with an immaculate uniform and polished boots. When he wanted to have some fun, he would get his motorcycle and chase the prisoners. "Go, run," he would shout, and then roar after us on his motorcycle. His idea was for you to run into the barbed wire fence that surrounded the camp and electrocute yourself. He kept doing it until someone got killed. He did it several times a day. After a while, it became hard not to get caught in the chase. If he got close, he would run you over. Then, if you could not get up, the German guards would beat you.

In the beginning we didn't even know that the fence was electrified. We didn't know. But we soon learned. It was just their way of having their fun every day. Many inmates got killed. It was the Germans' form of entertainment.

We also were to learn later that Auschwitz was actually three camps in one. There was a concentration camp, a killing center, and a complex of slave labor camps. I do not know which one we were in. To this day I do not know.

According to data from the U.S. Holocaust Memorial Museum, Auschwitz and its satellite camps were in a closed zone of nineteen square miles guarded by up to six thousand men in twelve companies of SS Death's Head units. The Death's Head personnel, who had been in charge of concentration camps since 1934, wore a skull-and-bones insignia on their black shirts and caps.

The three major units of Auschwitz were Auschwitz I, a concentration camp; Auschwitz II (Birkenau), the killing center; and Auschwitz III (Buna-Monowitz), the slave labor complex. Birkenau was the largest and deadliest of all German death camps. More than one and a half million human beings were murdered there, most in the gas chambers. One million of them were Jews.

We were in one of those camps. On the other side of the electrified barbed wire fence there were more barracks. Each barracks had a number. I do not know how many barracks they had, just as I do not know to this day which camp we were in, whether it was Auschwitz I or Auschwitz II-Birkenau. The four of us had no idea because in Auschwitz we lost all sense of direction. We were like animals, without direction and without any concept of anything. I don't know how we were able to keep track of time. Yet we came to know when the Jewish holidays were. We also knew each day of the week. I don't know how.

That first week we did not act like normal human beings. That was the Germans' whole idea—to take away the humanity from us and make us into animals. There were no bathrooms, only ditches, and you had to stand in line to use them. There was never any privacy. At the ditches, you had no paper to wipe yourself. All you had for clothing was those pajamas. Water was turned on at certain times and you had to be there fast to wash yourself or you would not have any water.

This was all part of the process of making you live like an animal, think like an animal, and act like an animal. It was survival of the fittest.

Many of the capos and block elders were killed by Germans because they did not perform their jobs with sufficient cruelty. The Germans thought they could get somebody to do a better job. A better job meant that there would be more people whom they could kill. There was not a day that people didn't get killed from beatings—the capos were that powerful. The more killings they would do, the better the Germans liked them. While most of the block elders and capos were Jewish, there were non-Jewish ones who were convicted criminals—killers, literal killers.

Everybody had a number. You were never called by name, only number so and so, period. I cannot remember what mine was at Auschwitz. Your number was stamped on a small tag on those "pajamas" and each tag was a different color. Yellow was for Jews, red for political prisoners, and green for criminals—most of them German and Polish murderers. The most vicious murderers, ones who were so cruel that they became camp leaders to kill more people.

When we saw a capo with a green tag, we knew he was one of the worst because we knew he was a vicious killer. Those were the people the Germans made the leaders.

After a while we started to ask questions about the rest of our family. You could not ask the capos because their answer would be a forceful hit, one that would bowl you over. We learned very quickly not to ask them questions. But now and then there would be old-timers who walked by and we would ask them, "Where is our mother? What happened to our mother?"

They answered by saying, "See, there," and they pointed toward the chimney.

We said, "What are you talking about?"

The old-timers responded, "That is where your mother is."

We did not understand. We did not know what they were talking about.

"Where did the other people go?" we asked.

They answered simply, "There," and pointed.

"What do you mean?" we asked. "When will we see them? What are you talking about?"

"They're there," they said.

But we had no concept. Our minds could not grasp it. We did not believe until a year later that they had actually been murdered in the gas chambers. We could not comprehend, but that was the answer we got—"See those chimneys. That's where your mother is, that's where your sisters are, that's where your brothers are." That was the only answer we got.

Four or five days later the Germans lined us up for a roll call and said they needed people with different trades—metal workers, glaziers, carpenters, and so forth. Among the things that my grandfather had sold in our store were glass windows. I used to see him cutting the glass and, from time to time, my father did the same. So my father, my brother Buroch, and I told the Germans we were glaziers.

They also needed young people to go for some special work—I don't remember what it was. My brother Mendel was fourteen. We did not know if we should let him go. In our culture we were accustomed to ask advice. There was no rabbi, so it was my father who was debating what advice to give. Was it better to stay? Was it better to go?

I don't know how the decision was made for Mendel, but he was taken away with a children's group. We were hoping that he would be treated better, but we had no way of knowing which would be better, which would be worse. He was separated and, as we later learned, taken to Buchenwald. The three of us who were left became glaziers. We were about to be taken to Warsaw.

Prisoners in Warsaw

We were among prisoners whom the Germans intended to move from Auschwitz to use for slave labor. Large numbers of prisoners, almost all males in their late teens, twenties, and thirties, were being transported to work in factories and at other locations where the Germans were building installations such as underground hangars and factories. They paid nothing for the labor and provided barely any food. In return, they got laborers, although we did not produce much. But we were cheap and, to the Germans, dispensable.

We had been allowed to bring to Auschwitz only what we could carry. There they took away any valuables we might have brought. Before we were shipped to Warsaw, they gave us blankets and, for those that had no shoes, clogs or what the Germans in Auschwitz called shoes. The Germans were quite meticulous.

My father, Buroch, and I became glaziers and, as such, we went to Warsaw. But before we left, the "canada kommandos" at Auschwitz separated us from what little we had been able to accumulate. The mountain of shoes and eyeglasses later documented famously in so many photographs grew even higher.

We were given blankets, which the Germans knew we would need in Warsaw. I remember that, strangely, they were silk blankets. Take one or two, they said, along with the bowls that each of us had been using, but nothing else. Each bowl had a hole that we used in tying it to our clothes. Each of us also had a metal spoon. A bowl and a spoon. That was our survival kit.

We were transported by train to Warsaw, approximately three hundred kilometers northeast of Auschwitz. Along the way the prisoners were beaten without respite. When we arrived at Warsaw, a different kind of world opened up to us. It was a very large city, and we were in a newly created concentration camp.

Warsaw in the spring of 1944 was a city half-destroyed. The air raids of the blitzkrieg of September 1939 and the devastating force of the Germans in crushing the heroic uprising of the Jews in the ghetto between April 19 and May 16, 1943, caused tremendous damage. In the course of the Warsaw ghetto uprising, the Germans killed or captured 56,065 Jewish fighters. At its conclusion, the commanding German general, Jurgen Stroop, proudly wired his superiors, "The former Jewish quarter of Warsaw no longer exists."

When the Jewish resistance in the ghetto was brought to an end, the Germans decided to remove all signs that it once had been the place where hundreds of thousands of Jews had been confined before their executions. On this site Stroop began the creation of two concentration camps. He reportedly regretted that he had not kept more Jewish prisoners in Warsaw to work on the projects. So, according to historian Martin Gilbert, he persuaded Gestapo chieftain Heinrich Himmler to approve the transfer of several thousand Jews from other parts of Europe to build the first Warsaw concentration camp. It was established in the ghetto area on July 19, 1943, just two months after the termination of the uprising.

To that camp the Germans transported many Jews, but none from Poland. They were afraid that Polish Jewish prisoners might escape and, because of their ability to speak the language, melt into the countryside. So to that camp the Germans brought Jews from Lithuania along with Greek Jews, French Jews, and others. A substantial number of the French Jews had emigrated from Poland but were now considered French. Altogether there were about five thousand prisoners in that first camp.

Then a second camp was built and opened in 1944. It was called the Hungarian camp, and that is where we were taken. This camp was close to the notorious Pawiak Prison where thousands had been murdered and tortured by the Germans. In fact, the prison looked down on us. It was armed with heavy machine guns in tall towers that gave a commanding view of the area, which had been cleared of any cover or camouflage. The camp also was next to what had been the Judenrat or communal area. It was where the principal rabbi's house had been. Nearby there had been a number of synagogues. Most of these, including all the main buildings, had been razed.

One building that had been allowed to stand was used as the headquarters for the SS. When we arrived in Warsaw, the very same SS man who had greeted us on our arrival at Auschwitz, the one from our hometown, was there. I do not remember his name, although we grew up right across the street from each other.

We arrived on a very hot day. I believe it was on May 31, seven days after we had gone to Auschwitz. It was about noon and there was a roll call immediately. We were lined up and again stood for hours. My brother passed out from the heat. He started to fall, but we grabbed him before he could hit the ground. The Germans, if they had seen him, would have shot him on the spot. "Whoever is nonproductive . . ." they said. We grabbed him and shook him and he was able to stand again. He was weak from lack of food, lack of drink, and the trip from Auschwitz. The Germans didn't see him. We were given a work assignment and the next day went out in groups of one hundred, marching five abreast in twenty rows.

We were assigned bunks in Barracks No. 3. My father was in the lowest one, my brother was in the middle, and I was on the top. We were to be there until the end of July of that year.

In Barracks No. 3 there was a block elder with a couple of assistants. They were cruel, but less so than the ones at Auschwitz.

Among those in the camp was a German who wore a red triangle which identified him as a political prisoner. He also bore the number "1" on his prisoner's garb from his days at Dachau. It turned out that he had been a prosecutor of Hitler at his trial for treason in Munich in 1924 following the "Beer Hall Putsch." He was now an inmate like us and the most decent man you could ever find. He was tall and thin but, unfortunately, I can't remember his name. His deputy in the camp in Warsaw was a Czech Jew by the name of Mautner. He was an intellectual and a cultured man, very decent. Later he saved my life.

Our job was to go out every day and take apart the partially destroyed buildings, brick by brick, placing 250 bricks in separate piles. Some of the bricks were sold by the Germans to Poles. Others were shipped to Germany. There were groups of inmates who separated the bricks and other groups who cleaned them.

In the beginning it was not so bad in Warsaw, but that didn't last long. There were old-timers there who taught us some tricks, and we listened. The first trick was never to appear to be idle. If you were idle, you were going to be beaten to death. But if, on the other hand, you did the hard work the Germans wanted, you wouldn't survive. So you had to find something in between—you had to appear to be working hard but do all you could to preserve what little energy and strength you had.

You also had to find a way to "organize." That was the new word we learned. "Organize" meant to steal, rob, take, get. You did not say, "Go steal a wheelbarrow." You said, "Organize a wheelbarrow." Organize a piece of bread. Organize some whiskey. Organize whatever. Organize.

That was the word that was invented in the camps. You had to learn to organize. If you did not, you were not going to survive on the food that you were given. The Germans gave us only a third of a loaf of black bread, probably a third of a kilo each day. I think we got bread every morning or every afternoon—I don't remember any more. It might have been at night. At night you also got some soup. In the morning you got some licorice water and at noon you had soup again. That was it.

Occasionally there was a piece of horse meat, but only occasionally. The soup again and again was the same soup. There were some sugar beets occasionally and barley and some turnips at times.

I promised myself that, when I returned home, I would never again eat a turnip. I would never eat any barley. I would never eat any of those things because that is all we got—just turnip soup, beet soup, sugar beets, and sometimes on Sundays a piece of margarine. Such was our food. To survive you had to organize. You couldn't buy anything from anyone.

Then, as we were being marched to the work sites, we realized that there was still another way to get more food. There was a quota for what we were expected to produce each day. It was something like a pile of bricks or two piles of bricks from every three or four workers. We figured out that if we could produce more, we would be able to sell some of the bricks to the Poles. They would come in their flatbed wagons pulled by giant Belgian horses to load the bricks that they would buy from the Germans. We reasoned that we could sell bricks to the Poles even cheaper than the Germans could because the bricks cost us absolutely nothing.

The Poles would pay the Germans and receive a piece of paper allowing them to load up a certain number of bricks. There were guards here and there but not everywhere. When the Poles came to one of our piles of bricks, although we were unable to speak Polish, we were able to communicate by gestures. We made it clear that we would give them another hundred bricks but they had to give us some bread and a piece of this or a piece of that.

We learned that we were able to load those additional bricks and receive in return some meat, some cheese and, occasionally, even a bottle of whiskey. Whiskey and cigarettes were the most valuable commodities we could get. We brought them into camp and exchanged them. We traded whiskey for bread, bread for soup, and soup for something else. We discovered that this was the way to get what, to us, was very valuable—food. At the same time, we discovered ways to remove the bricks from the rubble and clean them faster so that we would have more and more valuables with which to trade.

My father, my brother, and I always stayed together. In that way we were able to let our father sit down at a job site while we did the work. Along with us, there were those seven friends from our hometown—ten of us altogether. We had been taken from our town together and all of us survived together.

The others were all about my age. You had to be my age—seventeen or younger—because males who were older were put in work battalions and shipped to the eastern front. I was the oldest of those in our group except, of course, for my father. At eighteen you were gone. Five or six months older and I would have been gone too.

We were able to manipulate and take advantage of just about any situation. Our biggest problem was how to smuggle the traded goods into the camp. It was so closely guarded by the SS that it might be described as being hermetically sealed. So we put items in our pants. You had to place them high up so that, if searched, you would have a better chance of going undetected. There was a special technique as to how to do it—by your belly—but it was difficult in the summer when there was never any extra clothing.

It was a technique we had to master to survive. Sometimes it required cutting things into small pieces and dividing them among the ten of us. This, of course, could not be done with a bottle of whiskey. To smuggle one of those into camp, therefore, was a major undertaking.

When the Germans "tapped down" prisoners, they usually did it according to a pattern. If they tapped down one man, we knew the next man was going to get by clean. So we were usually changing positions in and out of the line. We succeeded most of the time. If we didn't, we would be done for—they would kill us right there on the spot. There was no question about it.

But the risk of life did not mean anything. You were smuggling in order to survive, so we did not think about what would happen if we were caught. Also, it did not take us long to master the needed techniques to the point that my father did not have to work very much anymore because we were able to shield and shelter him. We did his work and, although we might produce a few bricks less, we always had enough food to eat and were able to share.

At that time we had fairly decent conditions with half-hour lunch breaks. They brought the soup to us in kettles and spooned it out. What you did with your allotment of bread, how and when you ate it, was unimportant. Some people ate theirs at night. Others left some for the next morning. There always was the chance, however, that before you ate it someone might steal it.

There was a constant discussion about when was the best time to eat the bread: "Is it best to eat it at one time? Is it best to divide it up and eat it at three different times? Is it best to eat it in the morning? Just what time is the best?" We kept changing our opinions about this. At times you would put a piece of bread under your head at night. But what happened if, even then, someone was still able to steal it from you? There always was a discussion about when was the best time to eat. Everyone had a different idea. It changed ten times a day. And we were always hungry.

Once I ate lunch at the work site, laid down, and fell asleep. I slept for quite a while and, when I woke up, I could tell it was too quiet. Something wasn't right. I looked around and saw nobody. There had been a sudden roll call and everyone was called back into camp. Supposedly someone had escaped. So the Germans had a roll call. Five thousand prisoners were lined up, but I wasn't there. One prisoner was missing and I was that one.

I had been sleeping for an hour or more. When I got up and saw that no one was there, I started walking toward the camp. In the distance I saw someone waving and calling to me: "Where have you been? Come quickly!" It was the block elder and his assistant. They were pointing toward me and shouting, "We found him, we found him."

They motioned to me to come faster, so I started running toward them. "Do you know what you have done?" they asked. "You're holding up many people from work. Where were you?"

I said that I had been at work. But they said that there had been an appel for a long time and that I had not been there. They had me move faster as we went into the camp and they motioned to Mautner, the deputy camp elder, and said that they had found the missing man.

"Kill him," said the camp commandant. "Shoot him." The rule was that if you tried to escape, you were shot on the spot. But Mautner, the inmate whose views were respected, said, "Let's do it later. Let's not keep all the others from working. We will be wasting too much time."

"I'll take care of him," Mautner added. "Don't worry. Now let's get the people to work."

That night he asked me, "What did you do?" And he gave me a couple of good lickings. "Don't do it again," he said.

My father and my brother had been very scared for me. They thought that this was it. But Mautner saved my life.

On Sunday afternoons we did not work. Instead, we had to hold concerts for the camp commandant, an SS officer. We sang Jewish songs for him. Some of the prisoners were musicians. Others formed a choir that included people from all walks of life, and they sang to the SS commandant. There was one Hasidic song that was his favorite, a very famous Jewish song, "Belz, Mein Shtetel Belz"—My Town of Belz. It is a town in Poland with a famous Hasidic dynasty of the same name.

At Auschwitz and in many other camps, including the Hungarian camp in Warsaw, there were concerts by prisoners who were nationally known musicians. All the while the killings went on. That was the German mentality. They tried to enjoy themselves while they carried out their murderous work of destroying the Jews. This dehumanization began from the day you were taken from your home and continued daily. It was very well thought out, not something that just happened. It was all very calculated.

It should be noted that the SS alone did not do all the killings. There are films showing the Germans executing prisoners as far back as 1939, 1940, and 1941, and in those films not a single SS insignia is visible. The killers wore the insignia of the regular German army, the Wehrmacht. Then, as the number of murders greatly accelerated, beginning in 1942, the SS, the Order Police (akin to the civil guard in America), and the Wehrmacht took part. You could not kill so many people with the SS alone. On the other hand, some SS troops, like those in the SS armored division, had nothing to do with killing the Jews. Those troops viewed themselves as an elite fighting group and had nothing to do with the killings.

The SS guards in Warsaw were pampered. They wore handsome uniforms. They were provided with whiskey, food, and women galore. Anything they wanted, they received. Their barracks were beautifully maintained. Each officer had a servant.

The guards had a practice of asking the new inmates which one was a doctor, a dentist, a lawyer. All the prisoners in our Warsaw camp were supposed to be in the construction trades but, all of a sudden, there were some who volunteered as doctors. The guards actually did not care if any of us were doctors. It was just a pretense they used to weed out people, to dehumanize them even more. When there was an inquiry as to who was a doctor, some prisoners would volunteer, and the officer in charge would say, "All right, I need some socks to be washed and you are going to wash them." That was the reason the

Germans had been looking for someone who would say that he was a doctor—to have an opportunity to humiliate people.

The guards also would look at your hands. The men who had soft ones, not callused, would be given the worst jobs. Because they were not the construction workers they pretended to be, the Germans would say, "Now we are going to make you work. Now you are going to work until you die."

Many of the Hungarian Jews who were later shipped to the camps from the large cities did not survive because they were intellectuals. They were unable to do serious physical labor. They were unable to cope because of a lack of agility and because of their mental attitudes. My father, however, who was forty-five years old, was in good physical condition. He was both physically and psychologically resilient and resourceful, with great experience in the methods required to survive. Because of this, he was able to cope with extremely negative conditions.

Toward the end of July 1944 the Soviet armies were drawing nearer to Warsaw. Their tanks were only seven miles east of the Vistula River. Soviet artillery could be heard constantly. One night it was so loud the noise caused me to fall out of my bunk. We stopped going to work. It was too dangerous for the guards to be out.

The Russians dropped paratroopers into the Pawiak Prison and they opened the gates for the prisoners to escape. Railroad traffic to the city was cut off. The mass of the Soviet forces was now just across the river, and they encouraged the Polish underground army to begin an uprising.

Long afterwards we found out that there was a debate going on amidst the Germans about what to do with us. There were ten thousand of us, half in the Hungarian camp where we were, and half in the older camp nearby. The debate was whether to take us to a crematorium and exterminate us, to shoot us there on the spot, or to march us somewhere else.

But construction of the crematorium had not been completed. So a decision was made to evacuate us, to start marching us out because we were still good labor material. We were young and healthy by their standards. I don't think any of us died in the Hungarian camp. Some prisoners died in the older camp because they had been there a year longer. But our group was still fairly healthy. Just before the end of July, we were given orders to prepare to leave Warsaw. All that any of us could take with us, we were told, was a blanket, nothing else. We had nothing else, so it didn't matter anyway.

A Death March to a Death Train

On August 1, 1944, the war returned to Warsaw. There was an uprising by the Polish Home Army, the underground, which seized the center of the city. Close at hand, on the eastern bank of the Vistula River across from the city, was the Soviet army. Heinrich Himmler had been directed by Hitler to bring in troops, including a brigade of German criminals and one of Russian turncoats, to put down the uprising. The Germans decided that the prisoners of their Warsaw concentration camps were to be moved away from the city so that their use as slave laborers might continue. One barracks housing three hundred inmates was left behind. I do not know why.

My father and I and some other prisoners talked. Should we try to get away and hide? The Russians were near. We knew it. We could hear them. We figured that all of the fighting would be over in a matter of days. But my father told us that it would be unwise to try to escape. He pointed out that first of all, "The Poles are not known to be very friendly to the Jews." Second, he continued, "You do not know the language. Where are you going to go? They will catch you right away."

"Then," he said, "there is the matter of your clothes. You are wearing striped uniforms. You have shaved stripes on your heads. You will not be able to run far. You will be killed."

We listened and we did not run away. There were several instances like this one when our father's advice was taken and we did not run away. On this particular occasion it became apparent to us that my father was right; the Germans had taken escapes into account when they did not ship Polish Jews to the Warsaw camps. They knew those Jews could blend into the population. They could escape, but it would be difficult for us.

We began our march on Friday, July 28, when the temperature was well above 100 degrees. Within a couple of days after we were gone, the Polish underground linked up with the three hundred Jewish inmates, who joined the fighting. They lasted maybe a day or two. The Germans counterattacked while the Soviet army remained stationary across the river. The Russians never crossed. Almost all of the former prisoners left behind were killed. Only two or three survived.

The reason for the Russian inaction was to allow the Germans to destroy the Polish leaders and the potential structure of a new government that would have been friendly to the Western allies. Years later I met a man, one of the former Jewish prisoners, who miraculously survived. We never knew why these three hundred had been picked by the Germans to stay behind. Perhaps they were to be employed in destroying the evidence that the two camps had been there. I don't know.

The cattle trains could not be used this time to take us away. Trains could not come into Warsaw because of the fighting and the sabotage of the tracks by the Polish underground. We were ordered to march, but we were not told how far we would have to go. On that Friday we had started to march toward the town of Sochaczew about fifty kilometers west of Warsaw. It was very hot. We needed water but, of course, there was none.

We were marching in five groups of a thousand each from our camp, with German guards in front and back. Altogether in the march there were probably about eight thousand prisoners from the two Warsaw camps. The Germans continually changed guards. Cars kept picking them up and dropping them off. They did not march as we did. They would march for only an hour or so and then the cars would pick them up and replace them with other guards. While each of the Germans marched for only an hour, we went on hour after hour.

When, at midday, we reached the Sochaczew River, we were the first group and we marched straight into the river to drink the water. All of the other prisoners followed us to the river. The Germans saw what was happening and began shooting. We were supposed to have been contained by the guards, but when we saw the river, we simply ran into it. That was what any animal would have done and we, by that time, were animals. When the second or third group entered the river the Germans opened fire. Then no one wanted to drink the water. The Sochaczew, which is a large river, was literally red with blood. We resumed the march.

That day we marched on a main road. My father advised us that our feet would fare much better if we walked on the grass alongside the road instead of on the hot surface. The advice was something he had learned when he was in the First World War. We did as he suggested. We still had our own shoes from home. I was fortunate to keep my own shoes until the end of the war. By then, of course, they were terribly beaten up. Before we had left home, our parents had new shoes made for us. They were made strong like boots. Our parents knew we would need them.

With us there was an older man from our hometown accompanied by his two sons. He was one of Viseu's intellectuals. He was much older than my father and was unable to keep walking because of his severe thirst. For some reason the Polish people along that particular stretch of the road were decent. They brought pails of water to us. The Germans, however, would not permit them to give any water to us. Some of the Germans, in fact, threatened to shoot the Poles if they provided us with water. Other guards simply emptied the pails.

We could not leave the line of march to help the old man. Soon he could go no further. "I'm thirsty," he cried out. "I can't go on." But a guard came over and told him to keep moving. The man's sons—one was older than I and the other was my age—sat down with their father. "He can't go on," they told the guard. "He had better go, or I'll shoot him," the guard warned.

The sons asked if their father could just rest for a while and were told that he could not. "Either he goes, or I shoot," said the guard. The sons pleaded but the German pointed his gun and shot the old man. It was the first killing on this particular march that I witnessed.

We marched until nightfall when we rested in a field of freshly cut hay. The thousands of us were spread all over it. The Germans then brought some water and food, and the prisoners reacted like animals. You grabbed as fast as you could. As a result, half of the water was spilled. The prisoners became even more desperate for a drink. Some of them, somehow, had money hidden on them, the equivalent of dollar bills. So the Germans started selling drinks of water for money. Some of the prisoners without money went so far as to pull out their gold teeth to get a drink. In some instances it was the Germans who pulled out the teeth.

The next day the march began again. It was Saturday and, again, very hot, even worse for us than it had been because now we had gone two days without water. That evening we again rested in a farm field. All the prisoners had spoons with handles they had sharpened. One of them began to dig with his. Then we all started to dig and saw that the soil was moist. We dug a little more, probably about a foot and a half down, and there was water. We immediately put our heads down and started to suck it up.

Suddenly it seemed that all eight thousand men were digging with their hands, with anything, and there was more and more water. The Germans went crazy. They didn't know what to do. They couldn't shoot all of us. So they just left us alone. Now we had plenty of water. We just kept drinking. Then we filled the bowls we had so we could have water the next day along the way.

Sunday we marched again. We were headed toward the town of Kutno, a rail center about 120 kilometers west of Warsaw, but no one told us where we were going. We just kept marching. Late in the afternoon on Monday, we were resting in a potato field when it started to rain hard. Soon there was mud everywhere.

It rained all night. Everyone was carrying a blanket, and the blankets became soaked. We discussed what would be best: "Should we sleep under the blanket, over the blanket, or between two blankets?" It was a rough night. Then, suddenly, we decided we would run away—my brother, my friend Steinmetz, and I. We had heard that on the following day we would be put on a train. This was to be the end of the march. We were to get ready for the train.

We, of course, had no watches. It kept raining so we could not determine what time of night it was. You just had to guess. We decided that we would definitely run away and hide, period. We did not tell this to our father. Our plan was that one of us was to wake up the second man and then he would wake up the third. I was supposed to be the third. But the first overslept and didn't wake up the second. So we didn't go. We had missed it. When toward morning it grew lighter, it wasn't possible to go. That was it. We had fallen asleep in the mud. But we were lucky. Unknown to us, some prisoners had run away during the night. We were still in the field in the morning waiting to go to the train. That is when we saw Poles bringing back the men who had tried to escape. For every Jew that was found, the Germans would pay a reward. They paid those Poles something but, luckily, did not shoot the Jews. The Germans were too tired.

It was August of 1944. Two months earlier Rome had been liberated by the Americans and the Allies had invaded Normandy. Before the month was over, Paris would be free. The German armies had been driven out of the Soviet Union and were in a slow, bloody retreat along a thousand-mile front from the Baltic to the Black Sea. The Soviets were at the edge of Warsaw. But we had no real idea of what was happening in the war. We had no newspapers, no radio, nothing.

Yet no longer did we have any fear. All we talked about was survival, having food for survival. Nothing else. Nothing meant anything. We didn't think about our parents. We didn't think about anything. Day and night, morning till night, night until morning, we talked about food, what we were going to eat when we were liberated and what we were not going to eat. We always said we were never again going to eat turnip soup. "I will eat this," and "I will never eat that," we said. All we talked about was food, food, food, food.

We never talked about fear. We had no fear. Fear was not part of our makeup. An animal really fears nothing. An animal just wants to get a piece of its prey. An animal doesn't think about anything else and we were no different, no different. By that time we were driven by animal instincts.

After we were put on a cattle train at Kutno—it was in the middle of the day we had talked about escaping—we began what was to be a four-day trip to Dachau. Again, there was no food and no water. People became insane. There might have been as many as ninety to one hundred of us in a car. I don't know how many exactly. We were piled on top of one another. We screamed at each other. We clawed at each other. One man in his insanity ate his own feces. Some of the men in our car died. One of their bodies was cut. Prisoners ate a piece of it, human flesh, raw flesh.

One day when the train stopped the Germans gave us canned meat, which was salty and would have made our thirst worse. My father said, "Don't eat it. Being thirsty and not having water is worse than being hungry and not having food." So we didn't eat it.

We traveled like that for four days before reaching Dachau. By then we couldn't even move out of the cars. The Germans had to push us out. Flatbed trucks were brought alongside the train just to haul away the bodies. I think that only about eight hundred of us arrived at Dachau. The rest did not survive. When we left Warsaw, there were eight thousand.

In August of 1944 the Germans continued to transport prisoners to Dachau. This lasted until April of 1945, just before the war ended. All over the German-occupied territories, prisoners were being moved into the Reich as the Soviets advanced westward. The prisoners who had been at Auschwitz were marched hundreds of miles from Poland to Bergen-Belsen near Hamburg in northern Germany. It took weeks. My wife-to-be was one of those in that march.

Did the German civilians know about all this? They knew. The "special" trainloads of prisoners were seen by them. There is no question about it. We went through their towns and villages and everyone saw us. The same was true when we marched. We marched to work every day in Germany, through many towns and villages. My wife, as a prisoner, also marched to work every day, morning and night, through the German towns. The Germans could not have failed to understand what they saw every day—skeletonlike prisoners in bizarre uniforms, filthy striped pants with a string or piece of rope holding them up, a flimsy striped jacket and a round cap. There we were, holding our enamel bowls, wearing crude wooden-soled shoes and, in the winter, shabby coats made out of rags, coats that did little to protect us from the cutting winds and penetrating cold. The Germans could not have mistaken us for prisoners of war—POWs wore the uniforms of their individual services, were relatively well nourished, and were not subjected to the debilitating and harrowing forced labor that we did right before their eyes, every day. There can be no doubt—they knew, all of them. The guards went home every night to their families, all of whom knew what their husbands and fathers were doing.

Dachau and
Muhldorf-Waldlager

When we arrived at Dachau, we went through the same process as before to disinfect those of us who survived the march from Warsaw and the cattle train. We had showers and they gave us clothes. We also were given numbers. Mine was 33,000-something. Everything was done very methodically.

Dachau was the first concentration camp in Germany, having been established on orders from Hitler in 1933, the year he came to power. In some ways the camp was meticulous. The tables, the chairs, and everything else were in proper order. There also was less pandemonium than at the other camps because Dachau had more experience in its operations.

Dachau had begun as a political camp. A crematorium was added but it was used only to cremate the bodies of prisoners who died in the camp. The camp had held many political prisoners, including Leon Blum, the first socialist and the first Jew to serve as premier of France. He had been arrested in 1940 by the Vichy government and was confined until the end of the war. Also imprisoned at Dachau was Kurt von Schuschnigg, the Austrian chancellor who unsuccessfully resisted Hitler's demand for Anschluss with Germany in 1938.

There was an entire barracks full of political prisoners. At times, when we were roaming around, we met with some of them. But we did not know their importance. Our mental state was not that of human beings.

We met many prisoners, among them the Greek Jews of Salonika.

They were well educated and had been very prosperous. In fact, most of the people of Salonika were Jewish. The city, which was the second largest in Greece, was almost completely closed each Sabbath. The Jews there had great influence in banking, commerce, and industry. The Germans occupied the city in 1941 and virtually annihilated its entire Sephardic Jewish population.

The ones who were taken to Dachau were very interesting people, very intellectual. My father became a good friend of one of them and they stayed friends for a long, long time. But the Salonika Jews also were cunning and shrewd, and we had to be very careful with them because they stole from us. They were quite experienced at "organizing." They had mastered it because they had been at Dachau for such a long time.

Many times when we were getting the soup and had a piece of bread in one hand, the Greeks managed to snatch away the bread. It just disappeared. Somebody might have a cap or a pair of shoes in good condition but, if they were put down, they disappeared. Then they were sold to somebody, a capo or a block leader, for a piece of bread or another bowl of soup, to get a better place on the boards that were our beds, or to get on a work section that was less backbreaking. The work we had was all bad, but some kinds of work were less exhausting than others.

We had no knowledge of the whereabouts of my brother Mendel. We had no idea. My father, Buroch, and I had survived the trip from Warsaw and were still together. After about a week at Dachau we were taken by passenger train to Muhldorf, which was a group of satellite camps about fifty-five kilometers east of Dachau and Munich. The Germans had begun to put much of their war machine manufacturing underground. For this they had giant construction projects underway in the Dachau and Muhldorf area of Bavaria. Hundreds of thousands of slave laborers were working on them. The camp in which we were confined, Waldlager, was in a forest and contained a series of small huts with slanted roofs made from corrugated cardboard. The inmates in each hut slept on dirt floors. Each man was given a blanket and a specific camp chore. There were several thousand prisoners at Waldlager.

When we first arrived at the Waldlager camp there were no killings because we were still relatively strong. Surprisingly, we had recovered quickly from the death march in Poland and the cattle car trip across Germany to Dachau. For a while we were quite sturdy. The weather was not yet too bad, so we did not suffer much. We were not able, however, to organize any extra food. Nevertheless, we got by with what we had.

Our clothes were still fairly clean, and we had not contracted any diseases. The beatings hadn't started, and the construction jobs were not yet hard. But, gradually, everything got worse. The rains started in October, and the roads became very muddy. It became more difficult for us to do our jobs. More and more we felt the effects of our lack of sufficient food. And the beatings began to come more often.

Most of the inmates' no longer had their own shoes. They had finally worn out and had been replaced with wooden ones. Our clothes, including our underwear, also had worn out. So we were given paper shirts and paper underpants. They were made of rough paper, like grocery bags.

We had a daily work routine. There was a concrete-mixing machine with a ramp leading up to it. We had to carry fifty-kilo bags of cement up that ramp and throw the contents into a hopper, where they were mixed with water and gravel to make concrete. We carried the cement bags in twelve-hour shifts. We were not allowed to stop. If you dropped, somebody grabbed you, and you were either beaten or killed and someone else was put in your place.

The capos stood there to make sure you didn't slack off because, if you moved slowly, the machine would not have a sufficient amount of cement. You had to keep carrying those sacks throughout the entire shift. You couldn't stop even to go to a latrine. You carried a sack up one ramp and then you went down another to get more. This went on for twelve consecutive hours. You were always covered with cement, and you constantly inhaled the dust.

The manpower had to be continually replenished. Few people could survive there any length of time. We knew, therefore, that if we stayed at that assigned job, we were not going to make it. Other ways had to be found to survive.

So this is what we did. After the morning roll call and the licorice water, we were supposed to line up for the march to the work site. We decided not to go. How was this done? The trick was to line up in the right place. You didn't want to be near the end of the line because they knew that those people wanted to slough off and so they grabbed them right away. The same was true about the ones who were in the front of the line. They were grabbed. So your chances were much better if you were in the middle of the line, say, the third or fourth row. But everyone knew that, so everyone wanted to be there. There was much pushing and shoving. But it was worth it because, if you went out to the usual work assignment, you would never make it.

Once in a while I was caught. So was my brother. So was our father, but we saved him. Even when he was caught, we made sure that someone was quickly pushed into the line to take his place.

As fall came and it started to get cold, men began to die. At the same time, the work grew harder. The capos were cruel. At Waldlager, almost all of the capos were Jews. One of them, a little guy who was a Dutch Jew, was called "Al Capone." He was as cruel as he could be.

The work became harder, but by that time we were becoming more experienced at not doing any of it. Meanwhile, the food problem became more acute. We were losing any physical strength we had left because of the lack of food. There was nothing in the camp to "organize." All we had to eat was the meager food that the Germans gave us. My father, my brother, and I did not steal food from other inmates there. Some of the other inmates did, but I don't know of anyone in our group who stole. From time to time, however, we lost some of our food—pieces of bread, for example, that were stolen by other inmates.

As the weather grew colder, we increased our determination not to follow all the work routines. The schedule called for us to spend about an hour each morning and evening marching to and from our assigned work site. Two hours of marching each day. During the good weather, that wasn't so bad. But when it was very cold, those marches became intolerable.

We learned various techniques to survive. One of them worked like this. When we left camp early each morning at 5 A.M., it was still dark. Every morning each of us was given a one-inch-square piece of paper, a ticket that we were supposed to turn in later for lunch. With that ticket, we would stand in line to get a bowl of soup.

We always marched in groups of a hundred, five in a row, with a German guard in front and another at the rear. A capo would also be in front. An inmate in the front row would be given five of those pieces of paper, each of which bore a stamp, and he would give one to each of the other men in the row. I, however, had been able to get a razor blade to make a small counterfeit stamp to match the tickets. Then, a group of us always managed to get into the first rows where we would be given the real lunch tickets but would pass along to the other prisoners counterfeit ones made with paper I was able to get hold of. With this scheme, our group was able to accumulate more tickets so we could get extra soup.

After a while, however, the Germans figured out that more tickets were being turned in than had been handed out. As a result, they changed the color of the paper. It took us a while to find the same color paper, but we did. We always were able to come up with new methods to achieve our schemes until we no longer went out on that work detail—which was fortunate for us.

Helping us to survive at some crucial moments was an older man, a Jew named Einhorn who, years before, had lost an arm when he was thrown off a train in Romania. He had an artificial limb but later lucked out at Auschwitz because, apparently, it went undetected. Otherwise he would have been exterminated for his physical disability. Somehow he was able to survive the inspection at Auschwitz and eventually became what the Germans called a policeman in our camp in the Muhldorf group. It was Einhorn who knew in advance what color paper was going to be used the next day for the lunch tickets and who provided some of it to us.

By the time our scheme to get more soup fell through, the weather had become freezing. We continued, however, to find ways to avoid the work details.

The underground project to which we were assigned included the construction of giant airplane hangars that were supposed to be air-raid-proof, with walls and ceilings that were reported to be twenty meters thick. The site was operated by the Todt Organization, which did the armaments work for the German military, including the construction of various factories and military warehouses. After Todt was killed, Albert Speer took over the direction of this organized enslavement. The Todt Organization's supervisors were dressed in quasi-military uniforms, with black or brown pants, khaki jackets, caps with peaks, and armbands. They were the ones who directed the work provided by the inmates from the camps.

To do this work, the Germans amassed huge numbers of slave laborers, including not only Jews but also Russians and prisoners of war from many different nations. We, however, had no exposure to any of the others. We could see different groups at the construction sites, but we were never together. In fact, the sites were so big that it would have been very difficult for the different groups to mingle. We were supposed to do our jobs and the other prisoners theirs.

In our camp there were many prisoners in addition to those of us who had been brought from Warsaw. Some were German criminals, identified by red triangles on their prison uniforms. Quite a few were Polish Jews who had emigrated to France and Belgium. They had been prisoners for some time and could be described as barbaric. As such, they were well trained. It was from that group that capos and block elders were appointed. The capos were not satisfied just to survive. They wanted to have more food, whiskey, clothes, more of everything they could get.

As a capo or block elder, you did not pick up barbarism suddenly. You only came to master it after a while. Then you became an expert. They became more savage as time went on; the crueler they were, the better their chances of surviving. They had an innate tendency to be barbaric; now, in this unspeakable place, they had an opportunity to manifest it. But it was not enough to treat prisoners savagely; the capos also robbed their victims of any of the pitiful possessions that they desired.

As leaders, the capos and block elders wanted to do more than survive. So what they did was get those things they wanted, the food, cigarettes, whiskey, or better clothes, from other inmates. There was a lot of trading. From time to time the inmates were able to trade at the construction sites and bring back what they had obtained to trade with the block elders and capos in the camp.

There were, of course, various ways for the block elders and capos to get what they wanted. If someone, for example, had a sweater that they wanted, they either beat him, or just took it away, or even killed him—which was not unusual. Or they traded something for it. Perhaps they would give the sweater's owner a little more food.

Some items of clothing were actually made in the camps. There were plenty of inmates who were tailors. What determined whether you had reached the pinnacle of power, however, was the type of cap you might wear. The capos and the block elders were allowed to have civilian-type caps. I don't know why. So some of them made, or had made for them, fancy caps with braid and what they thought were more stylish peaks.

The truth is that no capo or block elder was an intellectual. The capos did not think. Everything they did was reflexive. When a capo saw a German coming, either an SS or a soldier of the Wehrmacht, the first thing he would do was grab somebody and start hitting him. That was how they looked like they were doing their job.

If you asked them something, they would not answer you. Instead, they beat you, and they always beat you in a part of your body that they knew would hurt very much, cause you to keel over, or even die. With one or two strategically placed blows they actually killed people. It happened many, many times, especially with prisoners in weakened conditions.

None of the capos had any sense of morality. If they had it at one time, it was long gone. The only thing they had was their power base. For a block elder, this included having a couple of people working for him. This meant, of course, that he had to support those people. How did he do it? He used food.

The block elder was in control of the kettles with the soup and its distribution. He measured out with a ladle. If he put a little bit less in a prisoner's bowl, there was more left over to give to his underlings. That is how he created his power, and this was the power of life and death.

With late September and early October came the Jewish holidays. Among us at the time were some outstanding scholars. One of them was Rabbi Yekusiel Yehuda Halberstam, a great rabbi. He was a rabbi in the city of Klausenburg (also called Cluj) in Romania. He came from the town of Rybnik in Polish Galicia and was the son-in-law of the rabbi of Sighet. A very learned man, the Klausenburger Rabbi, by the age of thirteen, was already considered a genius. During the war his wife and ten of his eleven children were murdered at Auschwitz. The eleventh child died in Auschwitz later, from typhus.

The rabbi had been with us since the concentration camp in Warsaw and was with us at Dachau and in the Muhldorf group. At the beginning in Warsaw we did not know who he was, but gradually, as he talked with us, we became aware of his immense strength in terms of scholarship and spirituality.

In Warsaw he had been assigned to the hardest labor. With about three hundred other inmates, he worked in the railroad yard where bricks were loaded onto trains for shipment to Germany. The prisoners stood in long lines passing one brick at a time to each other. They had to work very quickly, and the rabbi just wasn't able to keep up. Many of the inmates volunteered to help him but were not allowed. He suffered terribly.

This man, who was one of the greatest Jewish scholars in the world at that time, wound up with us in the Waldlager camp. My father told us we should listen to him because he had something to say. He would give us moral strength. We had no idea of that. When we started to discuss why this and that had happened, some people said there was no G-d. How could He tolerate what was happening? Some said if there was a G-d, why were we there? Those discussions alternated with our discussions of food. There were discussions of G-d, discussions of food, and discussions of what we were going to do when we got out. We never feared that we were not going to get out. We always had hope. We were encouraged to carry on because the holidays were coming and G-d would help us.

Rosh Hashanah Eve, 1944, the eve of the New Year, was on a Sunday. On some Sunday mornings we worked, but on most we didn't. Sunday afternoon was the time to mingle around the camp and talk. It was also the time to get disinfected and take a shower.

The procedure was for you to take off your clothes and turn them over to be put in a disinfectant machine that would destroy the lice. Each person had a blanket that also would be turned in to be disinfected. Some of the so-called huts were close to the showers; others were not. We walked naked from our hut to the shower place whether it was snowing or raining, no matter what. That was the procedure. When we got out of the shower, we walked naked again, without shoes. Then we were given back our blankets and we walked to get our clothes.

The size of clothes was not important to all of us. If they didn't fit, we were usually able to "organize" some other rags. More important were our shoes. Some of us still had our original shoes from home. It was crucial to keep them. Otherwise you had to wear wooden ones.

To have your own shoes was a necessity because wooden ones caused never-ending, painful calluses. Even with our own shoes, we obviously had problems. But what was important was to guard those shoes. Whenever the capos saw someone wearing good shoes, they would try to take them. If you resisted they would beat you or even kill you. So you did your best to make sure that your shoes looked dirty and decrepit because if they looked too good the capos would take them and you would end up with crude shoes with wooden soles.

I still had my shoes and my glasses. I don't know how, but they never disappeared.

On Rosh Hashanah, the Jews have a custom of eating sweet foods like honey. But where in the concentration camp were we going to get honey? Every three or four weeks the prisoners had been receiving pieces of artificial honey made out of sugar and, occasionally, some margarine. Because we knew Rosh Hashanah was coming, we decided to barter for honey so we could give it to the rabbi for a service.

The huts were in a semicircle and the rabbi's hut was near ours. The block elder also lived in one of them. In that area we were free to roam around. This meant that on Rosh Hashanah Eve anyone who wanted could go to the rabbi and get a taste of honey. Everybody, including the block elder and the other bad guys, went to get a lick because, somehow, they felt they wanted to be part of the ritual.

Then we had to say certain prayers. But nobody had any prayer books. So we said prayers by heart, at least those inmates did who could remember something. The rabbi, of course, knew all the prayers. On Sunday nights, however, you were not allowed to gather. You were supposed to be in your own quarters. Somehow, though, we were able to get to the rabbi's hut, and the prayers were said there.

The same thing was repeated in the morning on the way to work. The march took about an hour. Again there were inmates who remembered certain parts of the prayers and said them aloud.

The Jewish prayers at Rosh Hashanah are very spiritual, with great and moving poetry in them. Special books are printed just for those prayers. They include many songs. Everybody marching recited whatever prayers they wanted to say, with the guards seldom hearing them because they were only in the front and at the rear.

In Waldlager we always marched in groups of one hundred, five men to a row, twenty rows. When the guards sometimes did hear the prayers, they screamed that they were going to give us a beating, but we carried on.

It should be pointed out that by that time no one was really thinking about religion. You were not thinking any more like a normal human being. You didn't come to the rabbi for religious reasons. You came because there was a Jewish custom on Rosh Hashanah to eat something sweet. Some of the prisoners may never have been religious but they came for a lick of honey because, somehow, subconsciously, they wanted to be part of the Jewish traditions and customs.

Yom Kippur, the day on which Jews fast, was ten days later. It was on a Wednesday. The eve of Yom Kippur, which is the holiest time, was Tuesday. It is the time for singing the Kol Nidre service, which has a very haunting and emotional melody, one which each cantor sings differently. The Klausenburg Rabbi was the camp's spiritual leader. He knew how to bring out the meaning of that service and that prayer.

I do not remember whether we went to him for prayers that evening. I think we said them in our hut. Wherever we were, suddenly everyone started to chant the Kol Nidre. Everyone chanted it together. We were not worried about someone hearing us because in that camp at that time there were no Germans. They were all outside the camp. It was being run by the block elder and his assistants. In that camp even the capos did not have much to say about these things.

People like the Ukrainian guards were with us only when we were marching to and from the work sites. The camps were always run by the inmates. The block elder was the big boss and he had his two assistants. The capos were the ones who were in charge at the work sites. The Ukrainian guards were the ones who made sure that you didn't run away. They were the ones who would catch you, bring you back, beat you, and even shoot you.

On that Yom Kippur Eve we were not concerned at all about who heard us. We just kept chanting the prayers. I think the block elder even chimed in. He was bad, but we later received a considerable favor from him when my father was in great danger.

Wednesday was Yom Kippur with its custom of fasting. The night before we had received some soup and our usual portion of bread. On the morning of Yom Kippur we had the so-called coffee. At noon a cart was supposed to be brought out to the work site carrying a kettle of soup.

In the morning we did not drink the coffee. Then going to work there was a big discussion about whether we should take the soup and whether, if we did, that would break our fast. "How can you do it? A Jew is supposed to fast." On the other hand, we asked ourselves, if we didn't eat, how were we going to work?

The discussion continued at the work site. What should we do? We asked our father, who at that time was still working with us. Nobody came up with an answer. People kept saying that if we didn't eat something, we would not survive. Others maintained that eating the soup would not be considered a sin considering the condition we were in.

Then, lo and behold, as the cart was brought to the site, pulled by two inmates, it turned over and the kettle of soup was spilled. That was the end of our discussion. Nobody received any food that day, so we were forced to fast. When we returned to camp that night, however, everyone ran quickly to get in line for food.

After that, there were more and more rainy days, and more and more inmates became sick. As a result, the number of prisoners in our group diminished. It was the time when the Germans started what they called "selection" at Waldlager. The weakest inmates were taken to a crematorium. I think some were sent to Auschwitz and some to Dachau. By that time, in the fall of 1944, we had become veterans. We were together with the older prisoners, the ones who had been there even longer, and we knew what was going on. So we were aware of what "selection" meant.

The Germans had coined a new word, "Müsselmann," which they used to describe prisoners who were like skeletons, people in the last stage before death. The worst thing was for someone to be considered a Müsselmann. That meant the prisoner would be automatically pulled out and shipped to a crematorium. Each inmate, therefore, tried to marshal his strength so that he would not fall into that category.

In October, shortly after Yom Kippur, the Germans started to make their selections. They ordered us to undress and they walked back and forth looking us over. The men doing the selecting were so-called doctors, two of them.

"You go," they would say, or "You stay." They took down your number and that was that. Shortly afterwards they put you in a wagon and took you out to be gassed. That was the routine.

Meanwhile, the work groups were losing their laborers and the Todt Organization needed more manpower. So the Germans transferred more prisoners in from other camps. Each time they weeded out the inmates who were judged to be nonproductive, they brought in new ones.

As the Germans continued their retreat before the Soviet army, the death camps in Poland were being closed and their prisoners were marched or taken by cattle trains into Germany. Bavaria was becoming the main gathering place. It was to be the last part of Germany to withstand the onslaught of the Allies. That was why the Germans were building underground bunkers and factories there. Most of the slave laborers, the prisoners who were able to work for what remained of the German war machine, were brought to Bavaria. Our main work site was called Hauptbaustelle. It was the largest construction project for the biggest underground facility. Its completion was the Germans' first priority.

When we avoided going out to the work site we could either do work assignments in the camp or nothing. Nothing, however, was not wise. You really had to pretend that you were doing something, even if it was simply a work assignment that you created for yourself. You could never walk around without doing anything. You always had to have something to do. This meant that you might grab hold of a wheelbarrow. It didn't matter whose it was. If somebody left a wheelbarrow standing idle, grab it. It was yours. Or grab a shovel or a pail—pretend you were doing something.

Sometimes you pretended you were washing or cleaning or just doing something with a brick in your hand. Many times three inmates would get together, one with a shovel, one with a brick and one with a pail, and they would pretend that they were fixing something. Of course, if they caught you and found that you were lying about your job, they would beat you severely. If you were not doing something that appeared productive, you risked being grabbed because the Todt Organization's quotas had to be met. For the Todt commander, the soldiers had to produce so many live bodies. They did not care which bodies. And some of the Todt commanders were just as bad as the block elders, the capos, the Wehrmacht, and the SS.

In the course of time we were assigned to several work sites. To get to them from our camp you had to go through a town, sometimes more than one. We went in the morning and came back in the evening and always through a town. The German civilians, therefore, saw us many times, especially at night when they were in their homes or on the streets. There was no question about it. The German civilians saw us. They acted, however, like the sight of these ragged, starving men in their tattered prison garb with stripes shaved down the middle of their heads, all marching under armed guards, was very normal to them.

On Christmas we were worked only half a day. We could see the decorations all over town and the Germans could see us marching. There were thousands of us, many thousands, and the Germans could see us on Christmas Day.

Our camp was more isolated than many others, but it was not that isolated. It was only about four kilometers from Waldheim and we went through it daily.

There were four camps in the Muhldorf group and many towns in the area. Another close-by town was Amfing. There were many camps because the Germans wanted thousands of inmates to do their work. Consequently, there were many guards, and they belonged to the Wehrmacht. They were in their forties and even their fifties. There were no young ones. They were local people who lived with their families. The Germans saw—they knew. They watched us march, every day, a parade of starving, exhausted creatures looking more like skeletons than men.

The night shift was the worst. In addition to the backbreaking work, it was cold, very cold. Moreover, at night it was difficult to hide to avoid work, and you did not have any warm clothes. At the same time, you knew you could not survive working those twelve-hour shifts. I learned that very quickly. Nobody could survive those shifts on a regular basis—maybe for a few nights, but not continuously. So, when I was assigned to work on the night shift, I always looked for a place to hide.

Where could you hide? One place was the latrine. Another was to get behind a wall somewhere. Inmates kept disappearing and the guards kept looking for them. If they found you hiding from work, they would beat you to death.

At one of the sites I disappeared in the middle of the night, but I was caught and beaten mercilessly. Later I was able to run away again. I just wouldn't stay there and let them beat me.

The ten of us, including my father, brother, and the seven other men from Viseu, tried to avoid being at the same work site. We were able to determine which were the better sites and which were worse. There were certain places that were not as bad as others. So members of our group told the rest of us which ones we should try to go to and which we should not. We were able to switch.

There always was the risk that you would be grabbed and put on a work assignment that was terrible. So the idea was not to get caught for one. But there were not enough good jobs. Every once in a while, however, the guards came looking for a "specialist" of some kind. Once they were looking for a bookbinder. I volunteered, although I knew nothing about bookbinding except that once I had watched someone doing it. They took me into nice warm quarters that belonged to the camp commander. He had some books to bind, which he gave to me and said, "Go ahead, do it." I knew that I needed some flour and water in order to make a paste and that I had to have some paper. I asked for and was given them. But after five days the commander could see that I was not a bookbinder. I admitted it. That was the end of my special assignment.

The commander of the Waldlager camp was a member of the SS. He was a former teacher and, strange as it might sound, a decent person. After the war, at a war crimes trial, I testified on his behalf that he was a good man.

We kept trying to get assignments that would provide warmth and a little more food. We never were too successful as far as food was concerned. One member of our group, however, managed to be more successful than the others. He was my brother. Einhorn, the camp policeman, got my brother a job in the kitchen as a kettle-washer, which enabled him to get extra food.

The best assignment in the camp was to work in the kitchen. You got food there and were able to organize a little bit more—a raw or boiled potato, for example. It was very difficult to steal, but sometimes there would be an extra piece of meat or some other food. So, almost every day my brother was able to get a dish of mashed potatoes for my father. Buroch would give it to me and I would take it to our father who, at that time, was in the clinic called the "revier."

There were two types of sick bays. One was where they kept the Müsselmanns. Those the Germans felt could not work any more. These men had lost their will to live. The Germans kept them there either to die or to take them to "selection," which meant execution. They were given a minimal amount of food. They were naked. Each had only a blanket, nothing else. They were just waiting to die.

The other sick bay was the clinic called the revier. It was where my father wound up. That was in the early part of the winter of 1944-1945. My brother was still able to get extra food, which I gave to our father. Prior to this, we could see, when we went to a work site, that my father couldn't do much. Then he stopped altogether going out to the sites. We were able to keep him in the camp because the block elder somehow took a liking to him.

In addition to my father, my brother, and me, there were two other sets of fathers and sons in the camp. One father did not survive. The other lived until seven days after the war. His son is still alive, and I see him from time to time.

The block elder was shielding my father as much as he could. We were able to keep him in the clinic indefinitely, even though he was scheduled to be shipped to the sick bay which was for the Müsselmanns.

I was able to get near the kitchen to obtain food from my brother for my father. This was against the rules because you were not supposed to move from place to place. If they caught you, they would beat you to death. But I could do it because the block elder looked away.

At that time there was a lot of dysentery in the camp and many inmates died from it. There was no medicine available, nothing to treat it.

All the while my father continued to be the adviser. He advised other prisoners about what to do. The inmates from our town became very attached to him. He was the older person who people looked up to and asked, "What do we do now?"

My father, having been in World War I, knew how tough things could get. But he also was convinced that somehow we would make it. "Let's just do the minimum of what we have to do," he told us. He never was depressed to the point of saying, "What's the use?"

Meanwhile, the block elder helped us quite a bit. We knew that the "selection" would be soon and we had to make sure that our father would not be taken. We moved him from the clinic into a hut to keep him from being "selected."

At the beginning of autumn, after we had been in the Waldlager camp for about a month and a half, the Germans began preparing for additional prisoners. They built more of the huts with peaked roofs. They were located along ten "streets," each of which had ten huts. The inmates in those huts slept on the ground. When it rained in the old huts, the water came in and covered where you were lying. In the new ones there was straw to sleep on but the wetness was still there.

On each side of a hut fifteen men slept, or a total of thirty per hut. There were blankets but no pillows. At one end there was a stove. There was a door, but no windows. During the day, the door was left open to air out the place. The latrine was a good distance away. Surrounding each camp was a barbed wire fence. Our hut was on Street Number 3 in the new section of the camp.

Each hut was shaped so that a person could stand only in the center of the hut. When you entered, therefore, you took off your jacket and crawled to the place where you would sleep in the dirt. Your jacket became your pillow and, underneath it, so no one would steal it, you put your bowl. That bowl was really your only possession. Whatever small things you might have organized were kept under that bowl.

When the winter set in, we floated from one work assignment to another, trying all the while to get by while doing as little as we could. Once, during the winter, when I was returning to camp in the dark after twelve hours building the giant underground installation, I suddenly saw the camp's large spotlights go on. Spotlights were used for roll calls.

As I came into the camp I was dirty and covered with cement dust. I mean totally coated. I saw that the Germans were having a "selection." They were selecting people who were going to be taken to the crematorium. Then I noticed something different. Instead of getting the food in our hut as we normally did, it was there right in front of us. Obviously I was hungry, so when I saw that there was a line waiting for the food, I went straight for it.

That line turned out to be the group of men that had been selected to go to the crematorium. All the Germans did was take the numbers of the men who were in that line and that was it. Unknown to me, I was now one of those selected to die.

As I got my food, my father saw me and called out, "Oh my G-d. What happened?" But he already knew. The camp grapevine also knew it instantly—that I had been selected for the crematorium.

The guards gave my number to our block elder and told him that on his block he was to start with the selected men, including me. These are their numbers, the guards said. There were no names. If the Germans said that they needed three hundred inmates for the crematorium, they had better be delivered.

So I was one of those picked to be delivered a few days later. It was then the middle of the week. My father tried to figure out what he could do to save me. He went to Einhorn and asked for help.

Einhorn said that first of all I had to be cleaned up and given a shave. (Once every week or two we were shaved by a camp barber using a razor but with no soap. It was done as cruelly as possible. The razor was always a dull one that had never been sharpened. It was sheer torture.)

At that time I was unshaven and still covered by the cement dust. Even my glasses were caked with cement. I was eighteen years old, but my appearance made the Germans think I was ready to go to the crematorium. When you got through with each work shift, that is what you looked like. In addition, I was very thin. I was never fat, but by the end of the war I weighed only seventy-five pounds. Einhorn got me a new uniform and had me shaved. I remember that I had to wait until Sunday for the shave because that was the only time the barber came. Meanwhile, Einhorn told me that I should not go out to work for two days because I was supposed to be "quarantined" awaiting the crematorium.

After he got me cleaned up, he went to the camp commander and told him that there had been a mistake, that a healthy guy had been selected for the crematorium, and that I was needed as a worker. The camp commander agreed, and that was the end of that. Someone else was picked so that the Germans could have all their numbers. That was how things worked.

After the war Einhorn lived in Argentina and became very wealthy as a general contractor. He died not long ago in Israel, where I had seen him from time to time. As a camp policeman he never harmed the inmates. He was a very decent man in a terrible situation.

Another night, when I came back to camp from the day's work assignment, my friends asked me if I knew what had happened. "No," I said, "what?" That afternoon the Germans had made another selection to send people to the crematorium. As many as possible were immediately crowded into a horse-drawn wagon, naked, each with only a blanket. My father was one of them. He had been picked as one of the nonproductive.

But the block elder who liked him had heard about it. He went and grabbed my father out of the wagon, carried him on his back to our hut, and kept him there. So when I came home that night, that is what I heard. My father had been saved.

By then it was December 1944. The weather had grown much colder and the work was taking its toll more and more. Many died. Others were selected. Still others just waited to be selected. Our numbers were thinning out. It was at this point that the Germans brought in a large group of Hungarian Jews from deep in Hungary. They were young men in excellent physical condition.

These replacements, as they were called, were healthy and, when they arrived, well dressed. They were the youngest men in Hungary eligible to be drafted into the labor battalions, probably eighteen, nineteen, and twenty years old, and they came from different parts of the country. Most of them could have been described as assimilated Jews. They had had no previous contact with Eastern European Jews, our type of Jew. They were more intellectual and considered themselves to be patriotic Hungarians, not Jews. Nothing bad, they thought, would happen to them because they, obviously, were different from other Jews. They found out differently.

Until they had crossed the border into Germany, they honestly did not believe they would be treated the same as other Jews. They thought they would be treated differently because their fathers, grandfathers, and great-grandfathers had served in the Austro-Hungarian army and had been treated differently. These young men looked different. They didn't have beards. They didn't follow Jewish customs. They did not behave like the Hasidic Jews. They behaved like Hungarian gentiles.

But as they crossed the border, they encountered reality when, for the first time, they came under the control of young German soldiers who were anxious to beat up anybody. Those soldiers were free-wheeling. They had no discipline. Suddenly the Hungarian Jews were being beaten by them. That was their first exposure, a rude awakening. "What is going on?" they asked. "What is happening?" They were traumatized. They couldn't believe it. They just couldn't believe it.

While they were still in Hungary, although they had been taken away from their normal daily lives, they had been treated by their Hungarian guards as if they were special. They had not been sent as work battalions to the Russian front. They still had beautiful clothes, including coats with fur collars, handsome caps, and stylish shoes. Then they were brought to Dachau and the Muhldorf camps. They were told that they had to be disinfected. It meant beatings. It meant having their heads shaved. It meant having that stripe down the mid-

dle of their heads. And it meant giving up their fine clothes, clothes
they were never going to see again because they were "organized" by
the capos.

These Hungarian Jews had no idea of the procedures in the camps
where everybody stole everything, especially if it was attractive in any
way. I remember when they first came. They said, "We're going to be
strong. We're going to show you guys how to do the work and you
will look like Müsselmanns." We looked at them as if to say, "How little you know."

They still did not accept the fact that they were prisoners like everyone else. But it did not take long. It was not more than four weeks before they started dropping like flies. They had actually volunteered to
go to the work stations and carry the bags of cement. Because they
were still strong when they arrived, they were able to survive a few
days. But that was all. They had never done physical work. Most of
them were intellectuals who came from big cities, not from a rugged
environment. They did not know what hard physical work meant.
Many probably even had servants in their houses. They often were the
sons of fathers who did not do physical work, and they were absolutely unused to it.

One of the first things the young Hungarian Jews did when they
were brought into a camp was to look for their parents. They did not
know what had happened to them. They only knew that their fathers
had been taken away to labor battalions, and they were brought to
Auschwitz.

The young men also looked for people from their hometowns.
They spoke only Hungarian and maybe a little German. Unlike us,
they did not speak Yiddish. Moreover, they were isolated because, by
and large, they were dispersed throughout the huts. A few, now and
then, from the same town might be together, but not many. They were
not as cohesive a group as we were. There were hundreds of them in
our camp. At the work sites they immediately tried lifting those fifty-
kilo bags of cement. They thought they could show the guards how
good they were and that, as a result, they would be appreciated. That
attitude did not last for long. They couldn't carry those bags. No one
could.

At the Waldlager camp there was a continuing replacement of prisoners. The first to come were the Hungarians. Then there were re-placements from other camps. There was an assignment of French Jews who were brought in and an assignment of Belgian Jews. One of the French Jews was a man named Marcel. He was a short fellow, a nice guy. I couldn't tell his age because in this place the young looked old and the old looked young. He might have been in his thirties.

When the war was over, on the day of liberation, I saw Marcel sud-denly tear off a patch from the seat of his pants where he had hidden some papers and run to give them to an American officer. Marcel be-came the civilian head of the French occupying forces in our area. Unknown to all of us, he had been a high-ranking officer in the French underground. I would encounter him again under different circumstances.

There was a story about a young Hungarian who went to see an-other Hungarian in the camp who was a Müsselmann with lice all over his body. The young man would not go near the other man upon seeing him. He feared contamination. The man covered with lice said that he was a doctor. At one time, he said, he had servants. "Now look at me," he said. Instead of telling his Hungarian visitor what he wanted to know—what had happened to his family—the doctor just kept talking about himself. He was ready to die, and shortly thereafter he did.

Two days after his visit, the young Hungarian found himself cov-ered with lice. The same was to happen to all the Hungarian inmates. They had lice like everyone else. It took time for the lice to multiply, but not very long. I mean they multiplied like lice. At that time, I am sorry to say, lice were a major part of our lives.

Every few weeks we were given a disinfectant that killed lice for a day or two, but then they came back. This happened again and again, all the way until our liberation. There were millions of lice, and we constantly itched. They continuously sucked our blood. They were al-ways in the seams of our clothes. The only time their numbers were slightly reduced was in February when, to replace our cloth uniforms, we were given shirts and underpants made of corrugated paper. The lice did not stick to them.

Before that, we had been ripping at ourselves all the time, day and night, tearing at ourselves constantly. You were always itching, and you always had sores. You went to work with that all the time. At night, when we were trying to sleep, it was the same thing. The lice were always with us, all over our bodies all the time. With our hands we tried to pull off big chunks of them but, after that, what else could we do? To make matters worse, because we no longer had socks but only rags in which to wrap our feet, we got all sorts of foot sores.

There was snow and there were sores, and lice were on the sores, and all this was unremitting. The worst things we had to endure as prisoners were the never-ending hunger and the always-present lice.

Within a few weeks the Hungarian Jews were no different than any other prisoners. Some of them were drawn to our group of ten. They realized that there were groups of prisoners who stayed together for support. We were one of those groups. We always had our ten people together.

Since my father was a very wise man, other inmates frequently sought him out to speak with him. They knew that he never lost hope. From those new inmates we learned that the Russians were continuing to drive the Germans back. At work sites, people from our camp, including Polish, Ukrainian, Italian, and Russian prisoners, told us that the Americans and the British were advancing. Planes started to come over us—it must have been in February. We heard for the first time that there had been a landing in France the previous June and that the Americans were headed our way.

By that time we already had decided that we were not going to work, no matter what. All we would try to do was stay together. Try to survive. We would only do things we had to, but we would not go to work. This meant knowing where to hide.

There was another incident at one of the work sites. I saw a knapsack on the ground that belonged to one of the guards. He may have been a Ukrainian. I could see there was some food in it—some bread and a cucumber. So I "organized" it. The guard later went for his lunch, but it wasn't there. There was no cucumber. We had eaten it in no time. We had split it among us. It was the best food I had in a long time. The Ukrainian was furious that his cucumber was gone and almost killed people while looking for it. We never admitted what had happened.

On another occasion a friend and I were taken to a work site where we had to carry steel rods from one place to another. The temperature was below freezing and we had no gloves. My hands got stuck on the steel and my skin came off. Meanwhile, my friend saw one of the guards drop a watch. My friend picked it up. Later we traded it for soup and bread. That watch kept us alive for months.

You would trade something like a watch with the capos and the block elders in return for some cigarettes. Each cigarette could be traded for a piece of bread or some margarine, something that was a staple. For that watch we were able to get extra food for a long time. We shared the food.

By that time we knew that the war was coming to an end, and our main worry always was about my father's condition. He had developed phlebitis in one of his legs and could no longer walk. My father was in the sick bay with an older man who spoke nothing but Hungarian, which my father also spoke, in addition to Romanian, Yiddish, and German. The older man and my father had many theological discussions. "G-d is this," they would say, and "G-d is that." My father would say, "G-d is doing what He is doing. You do not understand the ways of G-d and you are never going to understand them." But the Hungarian was totally irreligious.

Many times I sat there and listened to those discussions. The Hungarian said that after the war he would become very religious but there was one thing my father would have to allow him to do. He had to be allowed to eat pork. He would observe all other teachings, but he had to eat pork. I don't know if my father ever gave him an answer.

The old Hungarian did not survive.

Toward the end of February we heard planes for the first time. We could see them flying overhead. They began coming with increasing frequency. Then one day we could actually hear bombs exploding. American B-17s had attacked the railroad yards at Muhldorf, which was one of the rail centers of southern Germany. All of the trains that traveled north and south or east and west went through that particular area, trains from Hungary, Italy, Berlin, and France. There were many, many tracks converging on this crucial point.

Aerial bombardments continued for two or three days, one attack after another. At eleven each morning, while we were at the work site, the planes appeared and started to bomb. The work site was very close to where many of the bombs were falling. We were scared and the Germans were scared. At first we went to the site and started working, but then, when the bombs began falling, we stopped. Start and stop.

After the railroads in the area had been bombed, trains could no longer move. The Germans desperately wanted the tracks repaired. I was lucky enough to be assigned to that work detail. One day we would repair the tracks and the next day the bombers would be back. So we kept repairing what the bombers kept wrecking. That was our job.

Eventually some trains were able to get through. There were tracks with railroad cars loaded with the booty that the Germans had looted all over Europe and were bringing home. There were, for example, hundreds, if not thousands, of carloads of tobacco from Hungary. But most of the trains containing this stolen booty were coming from Italy. They included carloads of sugar, rice, and grain. Because of the destruction caused by the accelerated bombings, most of the freight trains were unable to proceed further than Muhldorf. So we were assigned to unload the freight cars and carry the contents to trucks for transfer to warehouses. We opened those freight cars with the tobacco and, forming a conveyor operation with a chain of hundreds of prisoners, moved the tobacco to nearby trucks.

Our next assignment was to move sacks of wheat. Four of us grabbed each corner of a sack—I think it weighed about fifty kilos—and carried it to another truck. This we did over and over. We were also assigned to unload trucks and carry their contents into a warehouse, always under guard. They included SA security guards, NSS from the Wehrmacht, and others—all kinds of guards from various branches of the German army.

Each of us had a spoon with a handle smoothed to a point so that it became a knife. It could be used, if necessary, as a weapon to defend ourselves. Sometimes it was used to kill someone. On that first day of loading and unloading, we used it to cut open a sack of sugar and put the contents in our pockets. We also took some tobacco. When we went back to camp, we were rich. We had something to trade—sugar and tobacco. For a leaf of tobacco, there were prisoners who would give their lives. Smokers craved it. They would give up their allotment of food for a cigarette.

On that first day unloading the trains, I had a load of tobacco in my hands, but there were other prisoners who were going to return empty. One of the Hungarian prisoners, an older guy in his twenties or thirties, saw a piece of tobacco on the ground, picked it up, and put it in his pocket. Unbeknownst to him, there were three German officers behind him. I remember it as if it had happened only yesterday. The Germans said the prisoner had been plundering, and there were signs all over saying that for plundering you paid with your life. So the senior officer, a colonel, told one of the others, a lieutenant, to shoot him. They pulled the prisoner out of line and told him that he had been seen picking up the tobacco and that this was not allowed. The prisoner had not realized the seriousness of what he had done.

The colonel renewed his order to the lieutenant, but the lieutenant, who was carrying a rifle, was hesitant.

"Please don't shoot me," cried the prisoner. "I have a wife and two kids." He did not know that his wife and children had been killed many, many moons before. The lieutenant was told three more times to shoot him. Finally, he took his rifle and shot him on the spot.

But the prisoner didn't die right away. So the colonel took his sidearm and shot him in the head. All the while, as we were watching this, we had our pockets full of tobacco. We made sure that we emptied them as quickly as possible without being seen before we got back to camp that day. But later we continued to take some of the tobacco. This was the choicest job assignment.

Once four of us were carrying a sack of sugar. We looked around and saw that no one was looking at us. So I cut the sack in the center and we started to load sugar into our pockets. I was not aware that there was a guard behind me. He had seen me cut the sack. Just then an alarm sounded; there was another air raid. We dropped everything and started to run. Not far from there was a river, and we were running toward one of its banks.

The guard was screaming, "Where's the guy who cut this thing, where's the guy with the glasses?" He was screaming while the air raid was going on. "If he doesn't come out," the guard shouted, "I'm going to shoot all of you."

One of the Hungarian prisoners said to another inmate that he had seen me take off my glasses and that if I didn't come forward, he was going to tell the guard it was me. Another inmate grabbed him by the mouth and warned that if he didn't keep quiet, the inmate would kill him. So he kept quiet. After the raid ended, the guard was still unable to find me.

Later I found another way to do business. I was able to get another pair of pants in exchange for some item I had at the time. So I put one pair on top of the other and I tied the bottom of one of the inner pants legs with a piece of rope. Then I filled that pants leg with sugar. When I went back to camp from the railroad yards, I was able to carry a few kilos of sugar hidden in my pants, and I brought a lot of it to my father. He was still in the camp's clinic and was able to "warehouse" what I brought to him. My brother and my friends also were able to use the sugar to negotiate for more food.

One day I was returning to camp loaded with sugar when I was stopped at the gate. There was an inspection to find out who was bringing in contraband from the outside, and there I was loaded with sugar. It was after dark, the spotlights were on, and I thought, "What the hell am I going to do now?" They checked and they checked and I kept moving back and back until finally I found a place where the lights were not shining. I opened my pants leg and let all of the sugar out. Then I walked into the camp. That was a very close call. I had close calls a few other times as well.

As the air raids continued in April, conditions for the prisoners got better. There was more food (we were able to organize), and our workload diminished considerably. Our work in the railroad yards went on for two or three weeks. Finally a couple of tracks were repaired so that trains could move south. But hundreds of freight cars on the sidings never moved. By that time they were all empty.

The bombings became more frequent and more intense. The routine had been that we were marched to the work sites each day and at eleven the bombing raids occurred. At twenty minutes or a quarter to eleven, the Germans would start to run. They were far more afraid of the raids than we were. We knew, when the Germans started to run, that the bombers were on their way. At eleven o'clock, like clockwork, the planes were there again and again and again—literally every day.

This went on for several weeks and, eventually, we did not go out of camp anymore. It was too dangerous. Moreover, the Germans feared that we would use the air raids to try to escape. So we stopped going out. By April, we no longer worked. We also were better off because we were able to hoard supplies. We were trading the substantial amount of sugar we had taken. There had also been trainloads of wheat where we were working. That was helpful when Passover came later in April.

On Passover you don't eat bread but matzos. But of course we had no matzos. In order to make matzos we needed flour. So again my second pair of pants came into use. This time I was to fill them with wheat that I brought back each night from our loading assignment. I gave it to my father in the camp hospital. He was able to get a stone that he used to grind the wheat into flour. Then he gave the flour to a prisoner named Herman to bake into matzos. It was coarse, but it was very healthy. Somehow or other, Herman was able to bake in the kitchen at night. Nobody saw what was happening.

One of the responsibilities of our friend Einhorn was to keep an eye on the kitchen to make sure that nothing was stolen. He was the one who saw to it that the slivers of matzos were baked. The result was that on Passover eve anyone who wanted a piece of matzo was able to get it.

One night in April, I was preparing to go to sleep and talking with one of our group, one of the ten from Viseu. Another man in our hut told me that he was not going to make it. "It is no use," he said, "no use in fighting it." He did not get up the next morning. He died right there. His brother, Chaim Herman, who was with us in that hut, now lives in New York. He and his brothers-in-law are the biggest kosher meat purveyors in the world. Whenever I see him, he always talks about what happened at Waldlager and his brother dying next to me in the hut.

During those days, when the bombers came, my father, brother, friends, and I talked about being liberated and what we were going to do after liberation. We felt very good because we were convinced that we were going to make it. We just didn't know how soon. We were sure liberation was very close. We had no information other than what we could see, but we saw the fear in the Germans. At that time we had little contact with the guards, but when we did, we could see the fear in their eyes.

We no longer went out of the camp. We were jumping and dancing when the bombers came over every day at eleven. The planes flew very low. We did not know that the stars on the wings meant they were American, but Marcel knew and he told us. There were only the Americans, only those giant planes. We had never seen planes like that. In fact, I had never seen any airplane until that first raid.

We were elated. We gathered together to plan what was going to happen.

There was a prisoner in the camp who was a doctor. He was an uncle of one of the boys who were with us from our town. He also took a liking to my father. There was no medicine to speak of, but he helped look after my father. We saw to it that there was enough food for him.

All of us knew that the war was about to end. The Germans were going to close the camp and we were going to start marching. The rest of us were all able to march, but my father was in no condition for it. We did not want to leave him. "You know what will happen," someone said. "They will kill him." We knew we must take him along, but one of his legs was still in very bad shape. We took him with us, along with the Klausenburger Rabbi who had been in the hospital for many months.

There was a very large concentration of military in that part of Germany in the closing days of the war. Most of the German army had retreated into Bavaria.

We were ordered to begin marching toward the train station in the town of Amfing to the west of the camp. It was a long march. It was atrocious because we had no strength any more, even though we were elated. We took turns, two at a time, carrying my father part of the way, and the same with the rabbi. They would walk a while, then we would carry them, and then they would walk a while again. We had to be sure that when the guards got close to where we were, they would see that my father appeared to be marching. If they thought he could not walk on his own, they would shoot him.

I don't know how long it took us—it seemed an eternity. When we arrived at Amfing, we were put on a train in a cattle car. We did not know where we were going. Eighty to ninety prisoners were pushed into each car. We could see that one car had been loaded with supplies, including cheese and bread. Then the train started to move out. We headed west and then south. The war was almost over, but our imprisonment continued, and more than ever, our lives were in danger.

The Last Mad Days

The Third Reich was crashing in flames. On all fronts the German army was in massive retreat. On April 1, 1945, the U.S. Ninth and First Armies completed their encirclement of the Ruhr, forcing the surrender of 325,000 German soldiers. By April 11 the Ninth Army had fought its way across the center of Germany to reach the Elbe River. On April 27, Soviet divisions were battling ferociously in the streets of Berlin, and half a million Soviet troops encircled that city, ready to launch their final attack.

Everywhere the Germans faced defeat. Nevertheless, they were determined to use those last hours of the war to complete Hitler's Final Solution. At 4 P.M. on April 29, in his final act, Hitler signed his last will and testament, reiterating his faith in the German racial laws and his abysmal hatred of Jewry.

The crematorium at Dachau could no longer cope with all the bodies of the prisoners who had died there. When the Americans finally arrived on April 29, they would find thousands of corpses. The German plan was to take all the remaining inmates from the outlying camps and transport them to the foothills of the Tyrolean Alps, where they would be machine-gunned to death.

Between April 14 and April 27, the Germans began the death march of twenty thousand prisoners from the complex of Dachau camps. Some of these prisoners were on foot, some were in cattle trains headed toward the Alps. My father, Buroch, and I were on a train. We did not know it at first, but soon we realized that we were being taken away to be executed. Historian Martin Gilbert wrote about the journey of the Dachau inmates:

> They traveled by train while railway cars and tracks were being bombed incessantly by the Allies; they were left locked in railway cars in out-of-the-way places when the guards fled. . . . Whole days passed without an opportunity for them to eat or drink . . . terror and menace closed in on them from all sides. . . . up until the last, [the Germans] continued hatching their plans in the belief that they could go on executing them as before and dominate their victims, even as dominion was being wrested from their hands. Incapable of letting their victims go, they wreaked their vengeance on their prisoners precisely because the prisoners were even more defenseless than they themselves had become. But in the end nothing remained and they were reduced to scampering frantically about, searching for refuge like rats in a burning barn.

As the Reich collapsed, the railroad tracks in the area surrounding Munich were filled to capacity with trains bringing in the stolen booty of Italy, Hungary, Austria, and the rest of Europe, as well as trains carrying hundreds of thousands of retreating Germans, soldiers and civilians. They were all fleeing the advancing Allied armies, especially the Russians. The tracks could only handle so many trains. So the train in which we were confined spent several days moving from siding to siding, back and forth, to allow other trains to pass. On the night of Friday, April 27, our train stopped suddenly on a siding outside of Munich. We looked through the slats on the sides of the cattle car and sensed that something was different. Then we saw the Germans removing the insignia from their uniforms. Suddenly, the doors of the cars were opened, and the guards told us that we were free, that the war was over. Then they disappeared.

We jumped out of the cars and started to run toward a town we could see in the distance. "This is it," I shouted. "The game is over."

There was one car carrying food and supplies, and some of the block elders and capos had been in it. But now they were alongside our car, opening the doors, and we were jumping out. We seemed to be free at last.

A short distance away there was the small railroad station of the town of Pocking; we were about thirty kilometers south of Munich. We started to run toward it, but my father called to us to wait. "Let's not run," he said. "The first thing we have to do is get some food. Let's go back."

Meanwhile, many of the prisoners had started to run through a large open field that was near the tracks. In the distance they saw the town. But my father said it again: "Let's not run. If the war is over, it is going to be over tomorrow too. If it is not over, there might be a counterattack. There is danger here. The first thing we have to do is get some food and see what happens." The ten in our group listened to him.

Meanwhile, thousands of prisoners from the train were running away. Almost everyone went except the ten of us. Our group stayed together; none of us ran. My father said we should get some bread. So we went to the car where the food was, and it was open. I took off my coat—I already had "organized" a civilian coat—and loaded it with cheese. My brother took the loaves of bread. Others grabbed potatoes.

We needed water to boil the potatoes. So we got two pails and began running to the station to get them filled. Suddenly we heard shooting. It was coming from about half a mile away. The fleeing prisoners had gone as far as they could and had encountered Germans. Now we could actually see the shooting.

My father called for us to come back to the train, which we did. Soon the Germans began encircling it. We headed for the first open car. I was still carrying my coat filled with cheese. Others were carrying the bread and potatoes. One of us had a pail of water. But now we were separated. Everyone ran to the nearest car. I climbed into one and closed the door. Now there were only a few of us together in the same car—maybe five. The same was true in our father's car. Then the Germans locked the car doors.

We did not know it at the time, but dramatic developments had been taking place in the almost-defeated German forces. In Munich there had been a revolt among the troops; some wanted to surrender, others did not. A portion of the Wehrmacht tried to take over the city with some success. The guards on our train belonged to the Wehrmacht, and they had received orders from their commanders to give up. The insurgents were able to seize control of two radio stations, a newspaper, and portions of the city for a couple of days, taking as prisoners some other members of the Wehrmacht.

Some units of the Luftwaffe, the German air force, of which there were a substantial number in the Munich area, battled the insurgents. It was Luftwaffe personnel, still obeying the German high command, that the inmates fleeing from our train had encountered. Many prisoners were killed. The rest were forced back onto the train. Meanwhile, the attempt at revolt in Munich was overcome.

We remained on that train on the siding for a number of hours while another crew was assembled to operate it. Then, at night, the train started to move. We were again heading south toward the Alps. Despite prisoner casualties, the train was still almost filled. In addition to our train, there were many other trains on the same tracks, all loaded with inmates from the camps. They were all being taken south into the forests of the mountains to be murdered.

On the next afternoon, Saturday, April 28, two British fighter planes swooped down and attacked our train. About two hundred prisoners were killed. The pilots must have thought it was a Wehrmacht train. During the attack, some of us took off our prisoner jackets and put them on top of our car. When I jumped off the car, I got a tiny shrapnel wound on my wrist. The wound was not big. There was only a little blood.

There had been occasions when German troop and supply trains were attacked by Allied planes. The Germans had placed prisoner uniforms on the car tops to trick the attackers. So Allied pilots were wary. But this time it worked for us. The British planes stopped shooting and flew away.

After they left, the Germans closed all the car doors with us inside and the train began to move again. A few hours later our train came to another halt. We were on a curve, and in the distance we could see shooting. Two trains had stopped ahead of us, and prisoners were being emptied out of the cars and machine-gunned. We were to be next.

We waited our turn. All of the prisoners on those other trains were being taken out and shot. But there were still delays. Troop trains kept coming in different directions. Our train and others carrying more inmates had to make way for priority traffic.

Then it started to rain. We tore one of the slats off the side of the car and stuck our bowls out to grab the water. With that broken piece of wood, we made a fire in the car and boiled potatoes. We had food but we still needed more water. Fortunately, we were able to catch some of the rain that dripped through parts of the roof.

My main concern was about my father and brother. They had climbed into another car, and I did not know if they were still alive. It was two days before I found out that they were all right.

During that time our train remained on the siding. We were now near the town of Seeshaupt, which is at the south end of a lake called the Starnburger See about twenty kilometers south of Pocking and fifty kilometers south of Munich. It was a scenic resort area where many German leaders had summer homes.

Then there was no longer the sound of gunfire in the distance. As the hours passed and our train remained standing, it became clear to us that there were no guards—no soldiers, no military, nothing. Somehow, one of us managed to open the car door. It was early on Sunday morning, April 29. A friend of mine and I dared to go out and look around. The other cars were still locked. Then we walked a short distance alongside the train. We were hungry. We did not have any more cheese or water and we were thirsty. We kept walking but saw no guards.

I called out for my father and brother. They answered from the next car, and we quickly opened it. Then we opened another car. We walked away from the train toward a village and came to a farmhouse, where we went into the yard and caught a rabbit. Then we ran back to the train, which was not far away, and gave the rabbit to our father. "Here," I said, "try to make some stew. I'll be back." And I left the train again. By this time more prisoners had come out of the cars. It was still early in the morning, before 5 A.M. There were no guards anywhere. All of them had gone. They had disappeared.

While my father was making the rabbit stew, three of us went again to the farmhouse, this time in search of some ready-made food. We walked toward the door and, suddenly, I took a look. Oh my God! A man was right on top of us. He was big, probably six feet tall, and wearing overalls and a helmet. The helmet was the only way I could tell he was in the military. There were no insignias, nothing, but he was carrying a large gun.

This is it, we thought. We had escaped from the train only to be captured by a German soldier.

Then the man motioned with his finger to his mouth and asked us, "Hungry, hungry, hungry?" He was an American. We were free. It was all over, we had made it, we were free.

At that moment the U.S. Seventh Army was headed our way. He was the first of its soldiers we were to see. We answered his question, "Ya."

Then he walked to the door of the farmhouse and knocked. A German in his best suit opened the door. It was Sunday. The German spoke English and tried to engage the soldier in conversation, but the American was not interested. The German, who we later learned was the mayor of Seeshaupt, attempted to tell the soldier how glad he was that the Americans had come, how good he had been to prisoners, and how he would do whatever he was asked.

The soldier did not comment. He said that all he wanted the German to do was "give food to these boys." The woman of the house, who had been standing there, said she did not have any bread but she could make some potato soup if that was OK with us. The soldier asked us if it was OK. What a question! He then asked the woman how long it would take. She said she thought it would be half an hour. Again the soldier asked us if that would be all right, and we said, "Ya." He told the woman to start the soup and that he would be back in half an hour. He added that if we did not get the soup by then, he would kill her.

The house was beautifully furnished. The soldier told us that we should sit on the sofa. We were hesitant. We were dirty, wearing rags and full of lice. The woman clearly did not want us to sit on her beautiful sofa and she grimaced. The soldier put his hand on his gun. She did not grimace any more. She saw that the American meant business.

We sat down and got the potato soup. No longer were we prisoners.

This photograph of me was taken in Munich in 1946, a year after our liberation. I had gained back quite a bit of weight and am wearing the same glasses I had worn in the camps. My coat is one I helped myself to in the house of the surgeon-general of the German Air Force, which we took over in Seeshaupt a week after being **liberated**. I came to America **with** this coat and wore it for many years.

Me, my brother Buroch, my father, and my brother Mendal. This photograph was taken in Munich in the summer of 1947 prior to my departure for America. Because Buroch was away at the time in the Fernwald refugee camp, his image was subsequently superimposed on this image.

VALID FOR ONE JOURNEY ONLY
CERTICATE OF IDENTITY IN LIEU OF PASSPORT 18631
AMERICAN CONSULATE GENERAL, MUNICH GERMANY

Date   July 16, 1947

1. This is to certify that   Rudolph TESSLER   , born at

Germany   Breslau   Silesia   , on   12th

of August   1929.   male   single

xxxx   , intends to immigrate to

United States of America.

2. He (she) will be accompanied by no one of his family

3. His (her) occupation is   no occupation

4. DESCRIPTION

Height 5 ft. 8   in.

Hair brown Eyes blue

Distinguishing marks or features:

None

5. He (she) solemnly declares that he has never committed nor has he been convicted of any crime except as follows

xxxx

6. He is unable to produce birth certificate, marriage license, divorce papers and / or police record for the following reason(s)   xxxx

I hereby certify that the above are true facts, proper photograph and description of Myself.

Subscribed and sworn to before me this 16th day of 1947

July 16, 1947

No. 11659

This document enabled me to come to the United States in 1947.

The caption for this photograph, which appeared in a New York newspaper in 1949, read: "Separated through two wars, Isadore Tessler, left, 88-15 179th Street, Jamaica, and his brother, Salomon, of Munich, Germany, are together again—for good. Salomon Tessler came to this country under the Displaced Persons Act. His first comment was: 'Everyone is so kind.'" The photograph was taken when my father arrived in New York and was greeted by my Uncle Isadore. Actually, they had never seen each other before. Uncle Isadore left Viseu for America before my father was born. At the time of this photograph, my father was fifty-one.

I was working as
a waiter in Florida
when this photo
was taken in 1948.

Mendel, in his working
clothes, and me at our
New Jersey farm.

Edith and me in our wedding picture.

A bar mitzvah in Chicago. From left to right: my wife's brother Sandor; his wife, Reza; my brother-in-law Marvin Davies; his wife, Rose; friends Joseph Aranowitz and his wife, Manci; Edith and me.

My father and my stepmother at the wedding of our daughter Florence and Abe Mendel in the Palmer House in Chicago. My father was seventy-three years old.

Edith and me, our sons David and Mordy, and our daughter
Florence in Viseu during our visit in 1995.

The street and house where
I lived, as they looked during
our 1995 visit.

Outside my Viseu house, our family—three generations—was joined by
the woman who lives there now. She is at the far left.

Today, with no Jewish worshipers, the resplendent synagogue in Oredea, Romania, stands alone. The synagogue's beautiful interior includes its ark.

David and me at the tombstone of my paternal grandfather, Mordecai
Tessler, in the cemetery at Viseu.

Edith's father owned this building in Papa, Hungary. She and her family lived on the second floor. Their store was on the first.

This is the tombstone in Bratislava marking the grave of Edith's ancestor, the Chasam Sofer.

Edith and me in
Budapest with
the Danube
River behind us.

Rudolph and
Edith Tessler.

Liberated

American troops continued to advance into the area around Seeshaupt, and they released the remaining prisoners from the cattle cars. The prisoners were taken to the center of the town and placed in a large courtyard. There the Americans set up a field kitchen.

The three of us, the ones who had been in the farmhouse, had to look for the rest of our ten, including my father and brother, who were left at the trains. We found them near the kitchen established by the Americans, surrounded by food. My father's leg was still causing him trouble, and he asked us to move very slowly when he tried to walk with us.

Our father had told us we would be liberated either by the Americans or the Russians—we did not know which were advancing toward us more rapidly. He said that if the Russians were our liberators, they would not conduct themselves in a very humane way. In fact, they might well be cruel. They would give us food but, after that, it was not known what would happen.

If our liberators were the Americans, he said they would inundate us with food and we would have to be careful not to eat too much. That was what we had talked about prior to being freed.

Because his brothers had emigrated and shared many of their impressions by mail and by visits, my father knew something about America. He knew that its soldiers were going to be kind and probably would be handing out chocolate even though no adults from our part of Europe ate chocolate—it was considered to be something for kids. We had been told the Americans would have chocolate and that they would provide us with lots of food.

It took us a while to find my father and brother. All those cattle trains, which had been headed south with inmates who were to be exterminated, had to be emptied. There were thousands and thousands of prisoners who were suddenly free. Some could walk on their own power. Some had to be carried. My father had been carried from the train. There was total pandemonium. We were too exhausted to comprehend it. All we wanted was food, food.

We thought we were big shots because we had obtained some food from that farmhouse, but when we finally located my father and brother and the rest of our group, we found that they already had been fully fed and even had been given some cigarettes, something we didn't have. So we went up to the GIs and asked for cigarettes too. They always were generous. They practically threw stuff at us, too much in fact. Many people actually got diarrhea and became sick from overeating.

We thought the war had ended, but it still had about a week to go. We didn't care. We started to explore the surrounding area. We were free. We walked here and there and, as we did, we came upon actual fighting. In the distance we could see German soldiers with Americans nearby; they were shooting at each other. The Seventh Army was still advancing into German-controlled territory. So we returned to that courtyard in town.

We had no fear. We did not know what fear was. All we did was eat and eat. That is all we did that first afternoon. In the evening I said, "Hey, listen guys. Tonight I don't care what happens. I'm going to sleep in a bed. I'm not going to sleep on a floor."

We went to a nearby house, knocked on the door, and told the woman who opened it that we wanted to sleep there. She would not let us in.

But we were becoming more daring. We went up to a GI and told him what we wanted. He indicated for us to come with him. We did not know any English, and the Americans usually knew only a few words of German. In this instance we communicated by hand.

The GI knocked on the door and announced to the woman that we wanted to sleep there. "No," she said, "it's my house." "No," said the GI, "you don't seem to understand. You are coming out and they are going in."

"You can't do that," said the woman.

"You are coming out," said the GI, "and they are going in or I am going to shoot you."

With that, the woman went away and we took over the house. We went in and explored everything. Right away we found clothes. We got out of those uniforms, out of that underwear, and got dressed in our new clothes. But we did not take showers, and we still had lice.

That night we went to sleep in the house we had taken over. About midnight there was a knock on the door. "Hey you guys," a soldier shouted. "You are going to have to leave. This house is going to be the headquarters for the Seventh Army." There was an entire compound at that location. The house where we were sleeping was just part of it.

"But don't worry," we were told by the GI, "there is another house in the back." So we took some mattresses, put them on the floor of the second house, and slept very comfortably, though not in a bed. We stayed there a few days.

Eventually we also had to vacate that house because it, too, was part of the compound. The GIs told us to pick another house, which we did. Soldiers of the Seventh Army were the ones who had liberated Dachau, and they knew what had happened to the prisoners. As a result, they let us pick whatever house we wanted.

It took only a few days of being fed for us to regain our health and our strength. At first there had been a lot of diarrhea but, after a few days, we were OK.

That first week, the Seventh Army let us do whatever we wanted. "Hey, if you guys want to kill somebody, OK," they said. "If you want a house or something else, just kill for them. You don't have to ask any questions. You can do anything you want. Just make sure we don't know about it."

That was why much of the Seventh Army was replaced. They had seen the atrocities and were emotionally very disturbed by them. That is why they said we could do anything we wanted.

On May 8, 1945, while we were in Seeshaupt, the war in Europe ended. I remember it snowed.

There were many Russian officers who had been prisoners in that area. We met some of them; many were drawn to my father as a wise, older man. It was unusual to see an older person who had been an inmate and survived. Although my father in the spring of 1945 was only forty-six years old, he was considered an older person.

The Russians were not as gentle as we were. We never sought vengeance like the Russians and the Slavs. All we did was try to get food and clothes.

Once, when we were together with them, they said that we all needed some meat. So we went to a farm—the area was filled with lots of farms, although none of them were large. We went to a farm and one of the Russians brought along a machine gun. The Russians said to the farmer, "We want cream." The farmer said they couldn't have any because he was going to sell it. "You don't understand," said one of the Russians. "We want the cream." When the farmer refused to give it, he was shot right there on the spot. To the Russians it was nothing. Then they went to another farm. They wanted to kill a calf for meat. Again there was a refusal. So the Russian shot the other farmer and then shot the calf for its meat. An American soldier was with us. The Americans also shot German civilians. There was no order at that time.

As for us, we emptied several houses. After we were moved out of those first two houses because they were to become part of the Seventh Army's headquarters, we were able to get our own compound consisting of a house, a large barn, and much more. We emptied that house. Eventually we had suitcases filled with stuff—gold, silver, whatever we thought to be of value. We had many, many suitcases full of stuff.

We became friendly with the Russians who were among the first prisoners to be repatriated. Their repatriation began only ten days or two weeks after they were liberated. There had been an agreement made at Yalta by the Russians, Americans, and British that all Russian POWs were to be repatriated. As soon as they crossed the Russian border, the officers were shot and the ordinary soldiers were sent to years of hard labor in one of the camps in the Gulags. The Soviet government believed those men should not have surrendered to the Germans under any circumstances.

In the spring, most of the Russians went willingly. During the summer, however, as news of what happened to the earlier repatriated Russians began to filter back, there was desperate resistance by the former prisoners of war against being forcibly shipped back to the Soviet Union. In September, Dwight Eisenhower ordered an end to the American policy of forced repatriation but later, under pressure from the British, he reversed himself.

Many thousands of Russian prisoners had been in the Munich area. The day before the Americans began shipping them out, some of the Russians held a big party with all kinds of food. Everyone was invited. Our family, which continued to be together, was invited, but my father couldn't go. It was still very difficult for him to walk. So he stayed in the house and watched over our newly accumulated wealth.

When my brother and I settled down for the dinner, the Russians saw that our father was not with us. They asked where he was, and then went and brought him over. During the dinner we noticed more of the Russians disappearing. We did not know why. We later found out. They had gone back to our house and everything then disappeared. They were going to leave the next night, so they stole everything. All our wealth had been taken in a very methodical way by the Russians.

After we spent a few more days in Seeshaupt, the Americans decided that there were too many former prisoners all over the area and that a camp had to be created to bring them all to one place. So they brought us together and loaded us onto trucks. We did not want to go. We had it good in Seeshaupt and felt there should be no rush to leave. The Americans, however, decided to bring us to Munich.

Because a central camp was not yet ready, tens of thousands of Russian, British, French, and former prisoners of other nationalities, including us, were housed in a huge complex of apartment buildings near the center of the city. While we were there, at the end of May, there was the Jewish holiday of Shavuot, the spring holiday. We arranged for services in one of the apartments. It was a warm evening, and we were saying our prayers when there was a knock at the door. In came an American army officer, Captain Kaufman. He was from Brooklyn, spoke Yiddish, and had heard us saying the prayers. He wanted to join us. We said he was welcome.

Kaufman was the commanding officer of troops that had liberated Dachau. The soldiers under his command—there were about a hundred—were mentally destroyed by what they saw. They could not cope with it and had to be sent back to the United States. Kaufman himself became totally vengeful. He wanted so much to seek revenge that, after he was sent back to New York for separation, he returned on the same ship with a contingent of soldiers who were to serve as replacements. Dachau, by that time, had become a prison for thousands of the SS. Captain Kaufman was placed in command. He was, however, too harsh to the Germans and had to be discharged.

It was not the policy of the American occupiers to be harsh. Kaufman had begged his superior officers to make him the commander and told us that he had made the SS prisoners work around the clock, turning on truck headlights when it grew dark so they could continue to work. I don't know whether there were beatings, but he made the SS bury all the inmate bodies, and on and on. The Germans complained. They were SS. They were not accustomed to such work.

When Kaufman knocked on our door that evening of Shavuot, he was getting ready, after his discharge, to return to America for the second time. When he heard that my father had three brothers living in the U.S., he said he was going to find them and ask them how it was that they had not come to assist us. "They should have been here by now," he said, "and be trying to get you out."

He did what he said. When he went back to New York, he looked up my uncles and bawled out one of them, asking, "How could you do it? How could you sit there and not go to get your nephews and your brother and bring them to America?"

I had a cousin who became a New York Supreme Court judge. The cousin was sensitive to this issue and shouted at his father, "How can you sit there and not help your brother?" So Kaufman was effective.

As it turned out, my uncles had not known previously that we were still alive and had been freed. They learned about us for the first time from Captain Kaufman.

I later learned that another cousin had been a U.S. Air Force pilot during the war. His plane was shot down over the Ploesti refineries in Romania.

The military soon opened a large camp on the outskirts of Munich for the liberated prisoners. The Third Army was in charge; initially there was no government of any kind. It was totally chaotic. When some order was finally imposed, the people in the camp were grouped according to nationality— Romanians, Hungarians, Czechs, and so forth. We were not grouped as Jews but as Romanians. As Romanians we were not Allies, and preference was given to Allies. The French got preference. So did the Czechs. So did the Greeks. And on and on. We were considered to have been with the Axis Powers, so we did not receive the preference given to the prisoners from the Allied countries. But we were free.

Aftermath

The "displaced persons," or DPs, taken to Munich were gathered from all over southern Germany, all the way to Innsbruck in Austria. Those of us who had been in Seeshaupt were among the last to be brought to Munich. There we were housed in a compound that had been occupied previously by German military families. They were ousted, and we were given an apartment.

In one of the courtyards a kitchen was set up, and we were given ration cards for our food. Meanwhile, the Americans kept bringing in more and more former prisoners. The situation was total pandemonium. The Americans tried to get some organization going, but all we had in mind was food, food, food, food.

Gradually, the Seventh Army was moved out and was replaced by the Third Army under General George Patton. The replacements, who had not seen the atrocities of the camps, had a new and distinctive mission. They were to create a military government to take charge of Munich and the rest of their area of occupation with its entire nonmilitary population.

After Captain Kaufman contacted a couple of my uncles in New York, they began their efforts to try to help us leave. Meanwhile, most of us from Viseu decided we were not going to go home. For those in my family who survived, it finally sank in what had happened at Auschwitz, that my mother and brothers and sisters were no longer alive, that they all had been killed. Even though we were there and saw them disappear, it took a long, long time for us to comprehend what had happened.

Many of the other former prisoners were unable to understand until the end of the summer of 1945 what had happened to their families. For such a long time our minds had not functioned normally. It was as if we were animals, without any emotions or feelings. We never cried. We never laughed. It was many months before we could comprehend what had occurred at Auschwitz. Then we began to piece it together—the chimneys, the smoke, and the smell of flesh. All the killings finally came home. Finally, we put things together. We met with former Lithuanian and Polish inmates who had been in concentration camps for as long as six years, from 1939, and with Slovak people. One of our capos was a Slovak who had been a prisoner since 1939. By the time they were in Dachau and Muhldorf, those prisoners had gone through half a dozen camps. They were the ones who told us what had happened. Each of them shared their experiences.

I was not able to get back to normal until October, until after the Jewish holidays. In the months after liberation, our value system collapsed. We had no sense of day and night. We had no sense of anything, except being alive and eating. At the end of the war I had weighed seventy-five pounds; now I gradually began gaining my weight back. Most of us were barely functioning, walking skeletons. My father was in poor condition. Physically he was weak. Spiritually he was a giant.

Our minds were focused on doing what instinct tells you to do—eat. Meanwhile, the occupation forces tried to bring about some organization for the refugees who continued to stream in. They realized that hundreds of thousands of German refugees were also coming to the Munich area. Huge numbers had fled from the Russian front. Others had been expelled by the Czechs and other nations. Romania expelled them. Yugoslavia expelled them. Eventually they numbered in the millions. And they headed to Munich. It became a city of refugees from all over Europe.

On the outskirts of town the military set up a temporary displaced persons' camp, while a few kilometers south of the city they organized a larger, more permanent one. The camps the Americans set up were in a German military barracks. The large, permanent DP camp was called Feldafing. Ironically, it was located just west of the Starnberger See about thirty-five kilometers south of Munich near the town of Pocking. This was where our cattle train had stopped briefly during what the Germans planned as our death trip.

The Funk Kasserne camp on the outskirts of Munich was the transient camp. It was where the prisoners of war were housed—French, Russians, Yugoslavs, and so forth. The Americans gathered them there and sent them home to their respective countries. The ones who went home the quickest were the French—within a few days after the end of the war. Next were the Czechs, who had fought alongside the British. They, too, went home right away, as did the Yugoslavs.

Then there were the hundreds of thousands of Russian soldiers. They were in different categories. Some were turncoats who, after they had been captured by the Germans, fought alongside them in what was called the Vlasov Army. They were traitors. Russian officers came to separate them from the other Russian POWs. Trains came in every day and loaded Russians, but they were all kept separated, the loyal from the disloyal.

The pandemonium continued. The Americans tried to create a government, but it did not function. They kept housing all the people, feeding them, helping them to recuperate, and then they sent them home to their respective countries. I met some people who had been able to come from Russia because the borders at that time were open. There were no borders. No trains went on schedule. Only military trains functioned. It was chaos.

While all this was happening, we were in a temporary camp. It was near a beautiful section of Munich called the English Garden. The Americans did not know what we were. At first we were Romanians, because that was where my brother and I were born. Then we were called Hungarians. To complicate things, as the war neared its end and Russian troops poured into Romania, the country switched sides and joined the Allies, as it had done in the First World War.

The large Feldafing camp had tens of thousands of people, and many of the older ones were not well. The sick were housed together in barracks throughout the camp and had no privacy. There were about twenty people in each dormitory room. There was a shortage of housing, but there was enough food. The sick walked around in their pajamas. Some had sores. Others had a variety of problems. Quite a few died. In fact, within seven days after he got to the camp, a man named Hager from my hometown who, with the exception of my father, was the only father in our group, died. That left my father as the only father still alive.

Some of the former inmates died because they could not tolerate the food they were given. They could not control themselves. They ate everything the Americans gave them. They ate too much, and they ate the wrong food. My father always had told us that if we were liberated by the Russians, we would receive simple food—bread, potatoes, no meat, some vodka. That was all we would get. "You're not going to get sick from that," he said. But the Americans, he said, would throw all kinds of goodies at you and those goodies would be more dangerous than the simple bread and milk. That's exactly what happened.

Many died because they ate kinds of food that they had not had for more than five years. Many others died from illnesses they had previously contracted, despite the excellent medical attention provided by the Americans. In fact, the medical facilities were the pride and joy of General Eisenhower.

Feldafing became a very large camp. There were several thousand Jews there who had been liberated from concentration camps. Soon the population was increased by men and women who had survived by hiding, some in Hungary, but most in Poland and Russia. They had been hiding in houses, in woods, anywhere they could. They came west to Germany looking for family members and settled wherever there was a camp. Feldafing became the main one. It took many months before the camp had any working organization. The United Nations eventually provided some food and supplies, but the camp itself continued to be run by the American military. They provided guards—you couldn't just come and go as you pleased. There had to be some discipline; otherwise, there would have been all sorts of problems.

We did not go to Feldafing. We were healthy and did not want to go there. We stayed in the temporary camp in Munich. Our independence had started much sooner than anyone else's. In fact, when I went to visit Feldafing, I was dressed in a suit. People looked at me.

Wait a minute, they said. We haven't seen a suit in years. Everyone else was still walking around in prisoner pajamas. But I was able to get clothes almost immediately back in that house we took over in Seeshaupt. The only thing I didn't get was a hat or a cap. I still wore my concentration camp cap.

The temporary camp we were in near the English Garden section closed after the people who were there were repatriated. We were brought to the Funk Kasserne camp, which was still gathering former inmates and prisoners to be shipped back to their own countries. It was a transient camp. The Americans did not want anyone to be there who might be more or less permanent. We were supposed to be in the Feldafing camp. But we were able to talk our way out of going there.

We didn't want to go to Feldafing because it was too big. There was no privacy. At Funk Kasserne we had room and some of the trappings of independence. We got some pots, and my father started to cook. We organized. We had to. At that time there was no money. German money had little value. So what we did was get cigarettes and this and that, and started bartering. We would barter cigarettes, for example, in order to get some meat. Things that we didn't eat we bartered for other things that we wanted. We didn't want to go to that big camp. We felt that our opportunities for bartering would be severely curtailed.

Funk Kasserne was run by the United Nations Relief and Rehabilitation Administration. We talked with some of the people who were in charge and told them they needed to give recognition to the presence of Jews because they were among those being repatriated. There was no Jewish camp. The camps were based on European nationality. Later there was a Jewish camp, but not at this time. We told the officials that there should be Jewish services at Funk Kasserne. The Jewish people, we said, needed prayer services and they needed to have arrangements so that there could be Jewish marriages and other religious services.

But the camp authorities said there was no rabbi and that one would be needed for those services. We said we had a rabbi. "Who's the rabbi?" they asked. Our father, we told them. The ten of us from our town were still together, and nine of us made the tenth, my father, a rabbi. In our tradition it is not necessary to have a formal ordination for a rabbi. We accordingly appointed my father as rabbi to justify our remaining in the camp. We complied with the rules of the Allied authorities as best we could but changed rules as and when we needed to do so. We knew more about what was going on in this chaotic period than the Americans, and we had endured the terror and horror of the camps. The Americans simply weren't able to comprehend, initially, what we had experienced. But we did our best to follow the rules and regulations they promulgated. So they gave us an entire barracks, and we stayed there for a long time, maybe a year or a year and a half. That was our headquarters.

Although we stayed in the Funk Kaserne camp, we never sat still. We roamed and explored the countryside. Once we came upon a little village. It had a lot of vegetable farms, and we discovered that the people doing the farming were Swabian Germans. They spoke a different dialect from the other Germans, but we understood it because the people in our town were Swabian. It was a thick dialect, not as clear and clean as the regular German. Then we suddenly realized that these were the people from our town. They had emigrated to Germany with the men of their families who had volunteered for the SS. The families included the wives, sons, and daughters of those who had come and settled there in the late 1930s and early 1940s. They were people we had known.

In our particular DP camp there were very few Jews. Most of the Jews had been taken to Feldafing. We had a lot of Yugoslavs—Serbs—who were former POWs waiting to go home. We mentioned to them that we had discovered this village where there were SS men. They had thrown away their uniforms and gone home to their families.

When we told the Serbs about our discovery, they became very angry. "We've got to kill those guys," they said. How were they going to do that? "Very simple," they said. "We'll bring all the German men from the village in here, we'll see which are SS, and we will kill them."

Those Serbs were very rough guys. They were not shy about anything, and they were especially not shy about getting a little vengeance. They had a plan. Men from the camp went to the village and strongly advised the German men that they should come to the camp to be disinfected. It was a common practice to be sprayed under the arms with a disinfectant to prevent outbreaks of disease that could happen easily with the extreme heat and overcrowding.

The camp had a very large building where the kitchen and dining area were located and where all sorts of activities took place. It was to that building that the Germans from the village were taken. It appeared to them to be no big deal. Everyone knew of the problems caused by infections. "We will ask them to be disinfected," the Serbs said, "and then we will decide what to do with them." So they set things up.

While the women from the village waited outside, the men went in. In the dining area there were long tables. On one side sat the Serbs with spray guns in their hands. All of them were former officers. The German men, eighteen and older, had to take their shirts off and walk by. They were told to raise their arms to get disinfectant spray on their underarms. We all knew that the SS had their blood type tattooed on their left underarms. The SS men did not know the real reason they had been brought there. As they walked by, a couple of the Serbs began beating them, and the Germans never reached the end of the tables. They were killed right there. One hundred and twenty were killed right there. Then the Serbs got a truck and loaded it with the bodies and took them home to their fields and farms and dumped them there in the fields where we had gone earlier in search of fresh vegetables.

Just before this happened I had gone to visit Feldafing, which was about an hour's train ride. When I jumped off the train, I hurt myself a little and wound up in a hospital room together with a Serb who had been a prisoner. All of a sudden, he burst out, "You guys have to be killed!" I didn't understand. "You Jews," he said, "you have to be killed."

"What happened to you?" I asked. "Are you crazy or something?"

"No," he said. "You do not understand. You Jews will forget everything about what the Germans have done to you. You'll marry them. You'll do business with them. You will integrate with them. You are too liberal. You will forget all the atrocities. We will never forget." I assured him that we, too, would never forget.

The Red Cross and many other do-good organizations from various countries were working in the DP camps. Many of their representatives wanted to see Dachau. Surprisingly, they found that all of the camp's documents were still intact. Nothing had been burned. In fact, my number, 33,000-something, was among the records. The Germans had left so quickly.

Marguerite Higgins was the first journalist to enter Dachau, and when she got there with the men from the Seventh Army, the Germans were still shooting prisoners. The American gunners responded by picking off many of the Germans. It was April 29, the day before Hitler committed suicide, but that did not matter. The Germans were a machine for killing. One person, a group of people, the Nazi Party were not responsible. It was a whole nation, with few exceptions—religious leaders, officers, educators, intellectuals, professionals en masse. It was a policy, almost a theology. They were out to get rid of the Jews, to get rid of the vermin, "The Final Solution."

When Hitler started, he found fertile ground. The Germans were eager to be indoctrinated. They were the policy's instruments, and they wanted to be. There was never any kind of an uprising until the summer of 1944, and that was unsuccessful. Even then, it was not for the purpose of stopping the atrocities. Its purpose was to kill Hitler and avert the destruction of Germany. There never was any organization or any group of Germans who tried to stop the atrocities.

When Kristallnacht occurred on November 9, 1938, and Jewish property was destroyed or confiscated, most Germans benefited. There was no attempt to stop Hitler. At that point he was not as strong as he was to become. He could have been stopped. But the Germans did not want to stop him because they were envious of Jews. Jews were very influential in certain occupations and professions, in banking, finance, and other intellectual areas. While they did not control the country, they had an influence. Germans felt they would profit from the attacks on Jews. "We will gain that house." "We will gain their business." "We will gain their professional offices. We will gain everything." As a result of that belief, they went along with the policy. And I am saying it today. Nothing has changed. If Hitler were running today on a democratic ballot, he would win with 80 percent.

What occurred throughout those years, until the last minutes of the war when Germans continued to kill prisoners at Dachau, shows the hatred and the determination to kill Jews and the other undesirables. Gypsies were also killed because they too were undesirable. Kill them all and make it an "Aryan" race. The Aryan race needs to be pure. Kill the people who are mentally retarded because they are not right. If you kill the Slavs, that's all right too. It is all right to kill them because they are subhumans, "Untermenchen," in the eyes of the Germans.

As the Americans approached Dachau in the final hours of the war, we were being taken to be killed. They took us into the forests and, just ahead of us, they lined up prisoners and machine-gunned them.

At Dachau at least thirty-three thousand died and, even as the Americans arrived, the Germans kept on shooting and the crematorium kept on burning. They could not burn fast enough. During all the years of the Third Reich, nobody was ever shot or put in prison in Germany for rising up against the killings that were going on. People were put in prison for other reasons—for criminal reasons, for being Communists. But not one case can be documented to this date in which any German was punished for trying to stop the killing of the Jews.

It was not just the government. It was everybody. I have told the story about the officer who said, "Kill him," because the prisoner picked up a piece of tobacco. This was common. As soon as you got into camp, you became the personal target of a camp commander who drove his motorcycle to see how many people he could kill. And on and on. Killing was the policy. It was second nature.

When the Wehrmacht went into Poland, it did the initial killing. They gathered the people of the communities—the leaders, rich people, intellectuals—and they killed them right on the spot. That wasn't done by the SS. It was the Wehrmacht, the regular German army. That was the policy. Hitler enunciated it, and the German people accepted it, carried it out, and embellished it. Eichmann perfected it by taking hundreds of thousands of people in cattle trains to the death

camps. It was in the German psyche. The reasons I don't know. I can't
explain it.

When we initially arrived in Munich from Seeshaupt, we had no
prayer books, no Hebrew books of any kind, nothing. There was no
synagogue. (This was before the American JOINT Distribution
Committee came there.) We needed to find a tallit, the shawl with
fringed corners that Jewish men wear over the head or shoulders during morning prayers. We also needed a tefilin, which Orthodox
Jewish men put on in the morning for prayers. We did not have any.
My friend Steinmetz and I came up with the idea of finding a cemetery. We thought there might be a caretaker who could help us find
some old religious articles that were either left there or buried there.

We found that there was a large Jewish cemetery at the edge of
town that happened to be next door to the Funk Kasserne camp. I remember we went there on a Sunday. We went through the cemetery
gate and found the caretaker's house where an older German couple
lived. We announced ourselves, and they welcomed us. By that time
the Germans were very nice. They all claimed they had been friendly
to Jews and that they had even been hiding Jews. As a result, many
Germans got food from Jewish refugees.

Everyone pretended that he or she had been hiding Jews. Everyone.
They were the good guys. The bad guys were gone. "We were suffering and we hid Jews and we were friendly to Jews." What happened
to those Germans who were shooting us as the Americans arrived? I
don't know. They all disappeared.

During the first few weeks after the war, the Germans had not
known what to expect. There were Allied soldiers all over the place,
soldiers with all kinds of insignias and uniforms. The German civilians were more or less cowardly. They were staying away from us.
They were afraid of what we might do to them. But then they began
having contact with us one by one. They said, "Oh, I'm the friendly
one. Oh, by the way, do you have some bread? By the way, do you
have some cigarettes or some chocolate?"

So it was with that elderly couple in the caretaker's house. They
probably were in their fifties, maybe older. They were so friendly.

"Oh, come on in. Can we help you? Can we offer you this?" I said, "Offer me nothing. I'll tell you what we'd like to find out. Do you have any Jewish, Hebrew, prayer books?"

The couple were German, but the cemetery was Jewish. We asked them when the last burial had been. "Oh, a long time ago," they said. "There have been no burials here since 1938 or 1939. All the Jews are dead."

I asked again whether they had any prayer books. "Oh sure," the woman said.

Every Jewish cemetery had a building in which ritual services were performed. It was where a body, at times, would be washed and prayers said. Some of these buildings were large and some were small. In this cemetery the building was large. The couple took us into it, and we found some books. I also found a tallit, a large one. My father was to have it for many, many years. It was made of wool and was very heavy.

At that time we were still living in the first apartment complex and, when we returned, we told everyone we had great news. We showed them what we had obtained, the tallit and the books.

We were using those books when Captain Kaufman came to our services. He asked us how we were able to get them and we told him. Then it dawned on us. Something wasn't right. The couple had been too friendly. We began thinking. Munich had been a heavily Jewish city, a wealthy city, an old city for hundreds and hundreds of years. There should have been a lot of silver in that building at the cemetery where bodies were prepared for burial—ritual silver pieces including candelabra and covers for Torahs. They would be extremely valuable.

I said to my friends that the couple in the caretaker's house had been too friendly to us. "They were too nice. They told us where the books were right away. Let's pay them another visit."

A tram ran all the way from the center of Munich to that cemetery, and a few days later we made another trip to see the couple. "Tell me," I said, "what happened to the silver?"

"Oh," they said, "that was taken a long, long time ago."

"Where did it go?" I asked.

"We don't know," was their answer. "They took it away but we tried to save it."

"Now hold on," I said. "Who took it? When was it taken? Where was it taken?"

We could sense that the communication between the husband and wife was not comfortable. Each one said only a little bit. There was something about the way they were talking that caused us to think they might be telling us a story.

"Are you sure that is what happened?" I asked.

"Sure," answered the man. Then he was given a good slap and he said, "No, no silver." He was given another slap. This time he said there might be something there.

Suddenly, we looked around and noticed that one of the walls was different from the others. We starting hitting it and knew that it was false. Then we were able to open it. The space behind was loaded with silver.

We left it there and went to the rabbi in town, whom we knew, and told him about our find. A short time later, the silver was taken from that couple's house and given to what remained of the local Jewish community. The rabbi was a German Jew from Munich who became the rabbi of the small group of Munich Jews who returned from concentration camps. They established their own small congregation in the former Jewish community house in Munich.

At that time we had no sense of the silver's value. We could have taken it. There probably was hundreds of thousands of dollars' worth of silver there, maybe millions. We had no concept of value. We wanted a Torah. We wanted prayer books. That was all we were after. We would later get books galore from that house. The couple had hidden all the valuable things. They knew what they were doing. There was no question about it.

Right after the war there was a small Jewish community in Munich consisting of natives who returned from concentration camps and from Russia. Meanwhile, the Americans were trying to move the displaced persons to the camp at Feldafing. We were just about the only ones who remained in Funk Kasserne. We did it under the pretense that we were needed as a minyan. We did not want to leave the city. Then it became known to the refugees that Shloime Tessler, my father, was there. People came from Romania, Hungary, Czechoslovakia, Poland, and Russia, and they wanted to talk to my father.

We had plenty of room for them. A barracks could house as many as three hundred people. We had only ten living in ours, but my father always had an open house. Food was no longer the problem it had been. The only question was what kind of food. My father cooked. He was an expert in inventing some original dishes when we did not have the traditional ingredients. For instance, we had a lot of canned foods but no fresh products like eggs. However, we had dried eggs, and from them he made scrambled and fried eggs. He made many different concoctions from a few basic foods.

While we had a variety of canned foods, we were trying to get fresh foods. So we were continually bartering. Our main currency was cigarettes and chocolate. A carton of cigarettes could get us whatever we wanted. The German mark had limited value, so we didn't want to have it. The American dollar, of course, had value, but the main bartering currency was cigarettes. A carton would get us anything and everything.

There were still food shortages. In the beginning we helped ourselves many times to whatever we found in the stores. During those first few months we did not stand in line for anything. We did not take orders from anybody except the Americans, and they were very lenient with us. If there was a line for bread, we got first in line. The same for fruit and everything else. We were former inmates. We were D.P.s and we were not going to stand in line. Never. We did not follow any rules.

Then we got an apartment in the city. Apartments were being given out by an office that provided housing for the refugees. Those apartments, which had been occupied by members of the SS and functionaries of the Nazi Party, had to be turned over to former inmates first. We used the apartment to store goods that we sold and only occasionally used it as a place to stay. We stayed in the camp.

We decided we wanted another apartment, and we got one. But at that time, during the summer months, we became restless. We were beginning to get back our rationality. It was then that we realized what had happened to our family, and that we were not going to go home again. I do not know of any former inmates, except for a few Communists, who went home right away to their respective countries. We were never going to go home to the old country, we said. That was not even a consideration.

It was not a country that we could go back to. All of our families were gone. Everything was destroyed. We could not possibly go there, because the whole country was polluted with hatred and it would never be tolerable to live there again.

But we did not know where my brother Mendel was. We hoped that he had survived the war. We started to look in various documentation centers that the Red Cross had established. But we still could not find him.

Occupied Germany was divided into four zones: Russian, British, French, and American. We heard that in the British zone there was a large camp called Bergen-Belsen. We thought that maybe we could find Mendel there. Steinmetz, one of our ten, also found out that his wife—he had been married just before the war—might be there, along with his sister. Others among our group thought that somebody each of them knew might also be there.

There were no scheduled trains. Military trains were coming and going, but you had to have a special permit to get on one. We checked the maps. We knew that trains went from city A to city B and from city B to city C, and that eventually we could reach our desired destination. Again, we did not ask any questions. We did not wait in a line. We just went to the train station, went to the front, and got on the train. We didn't have any problems.

On every train there were military escorts, American MPs. We were refugees, DPs, so we just went. The Americans were very tolerant of us everywhere we went, very tolerant. We spoke German and began to pick up a few words of English. The Americans knew who we were. We were not dressed like Germans. We always told the Americans, "Hey, listen. We are DPs." They opened doors for us any place we wanted to go. We sat with them. They gave us cigarettes and whatever we needed, anything they could share with us. They were very generous.

We took food with us on the train. There were only a few stores open. They had nothing except what was being rationed, and the rations were very minimal. Some bakeries and a few other stores were open for a few hours in the morning, but they didn't have enough food even for the ration cards. So they were open for only a very short period of time.

We had all we needed until we got to Kassel. That was the first big city we came to in the British zone. It was a railroad center that had been destroyed by Allied bombers. By that time we had run out of bread. So we talked among ourselves about who was going to go into town and get some bread. Some of us were delegated to find a bakery, and we did. But it was closed. How are you going to get bread when the bakery is closed? We found out where the baker lived and went to his house.

He said, "Don't bother me. I work all night and now I'm sleeping."

"No," we told him. "You don't understand. We need bread."

"Leave me alone," the baker said.

But we couldn't do that. We needed bread. So we went back to the train and returned with a couple of soldiers with guns. They told the baker to open his doors and give us bread. So we got bread. That was the way of doing business.

The next day we made it to Celle, the town outside Bergen-Belsen. In Celle we split up. It was as far as the train went. Three of us hitchhiked the rest of the distance to the camp. With me were Steinmetz and a rabbi, a son of the Rabbi of Viseu, who had been with us in the camps. He was looking for his wife who, unknown to him, had been taken to Sweden just two weeks earlier. He had vowed that after the war he would not be a rabbi. But when he was in Celle, Steinmetz convinced him to reconsider. A local woman made a black robe for him and he again took on his rabbinical obligations. This rabbi would officiate at my wedding in New York a few years later.

Bergen-Belsen had been liberated by the British. British soldiers were less tolerant than the Americans. They were more stringent, more dogmatic. I think they believed that all the Jews were going to wind up in Palestine. It was no secret. Our aim was to go to Palestine, period. Some wanted to go to America, but given the quotas, the successful ones would be few and far between. This was true even though people like us had uncles and aunts there. We had little hope that we would go to America. We might have to wait for years. So we all wanted to go to Palestine.

The British knew this and, as a result, were more alert. In addition, they were very reserved, the opposite of the free-wheeling Americans. In a way, the British were Germanic. They never seemed to smile.

When Bergen-Belsen was liberated by the British and Canadians on April 15, there were sixty thousand survivors, the largest number of any camp. Typhus was rampant. Eight hundred inmates died from it on the very day that the British arrived. Many, many more were still to die from the disease. My wife's sister, Blanka, was one of them. She died about a week after the camp was liberated.

The typhus outbreak was followed by typhoid. Forty percent of the sixty thousand men and women alive when the British and Canadians arrived died in the following four weeks, mostly from typhus, dysentery, starvation, and exhaustion of body and spirit. For months there had been practically no food for the inmates and, in the final four days before liberation, no food or water whatsoever.

My friend Steinmetz found his sister at Bergen-Belsen. But his wife had already gone home to Romania to look for him. Another sister, who had been liberated and was seen in the Russian zone, disappeared. She was never found. I discovered that three of my cousins from Viseu had survived and gone to Sweden. I was able to learn this because a list of the people who were taken there was available. The Swedish government had invited hundreds of sick survivors to come to Sweden to recuperate as guests of the government. The survivors were taken there on Red Cross hospital ships.

At Bergen-Belsen I met about a hundred girls from my area who had been inmates of various camps. There were some members of my extended family who I knew had survived, and I asked those girls about them. They would tell me, "This one's alive. This one's not alive."

Those women were as traumatized as all the other DPs. They came from various camps in Germany, Poland, and elsewhere. Most of this group knew my father by name because he had been so prominent in our community and the surrounding area. I told them what I knew about those who had survived.

I was at Bergen-Belsen only a short period of time, a few days. Then I went back to Munich and continued looking for my brother Mendel. We looked at people in different camps but couldn't find him. We found that there was a town called Kham on the German side of the Czech border where there was a hospital. It was possible that my brother was there. I traveled to Kham by train and by hitch-hiking on trucks with another friend of mine, a man by the name of Ganz. We didn't worry about where to sleep. We slept on the tops of trains, anywhere. We didn't worry about anything. If we needed food, we went to a bakery along the way and got whatever we needed.

In Kham we found a hospital under American control but, strangely, it was operated by former Hungarian army officers as if they were still in positions of power. It was a beautiful hospital, but we had difficulty getting into it. We had to have visitors' passes. I looked around and asked what was going on. The Hungarians hadn't won the war, but they were still dressed in their military uniforms. I was able to get in and told the nurses and doctors I was looking for a Tessler. I found Mendel. He was in bed with a gunshot wound in his thigh.

Mendel had been one of the prisoners marched out of Buchenwald during the closing days of the war. The Germans intended to shoot the remaining prisoners, at least the ones who didn't die from starvation or exhaustion. They wanted to get rid of the human evidence— but they waited a bit too long, and there were too many left to be killed as the Americans approached. They were being marched south-east to the border of Czechoslovakia when the Americans got there. It was the last part of Germany the Americans reached in May.

I found that my brother, other than being wounded, was healthy. He was then fifteen years old. I don't know how bad his experiences were, but I think they were better than others. He had been shot when he was near his German guards and the Americans fired into them. His thigh bone was shattered. He had been taken to this hospital, where he underwent a couple of operations.

I said I wanted to take my brother out. "No," said one of the Hungarian officers. "You can't do that. This is a military hospital."

I said, "Hey you guys, you don't understand. You didn't win the war. We won the war."

I went to the American captain who was in charge. "You won the war," I told him, "and I am not taking orders from the Hungarians. I'm taking my brother with me. How the hell can you operate like this? Those guys are running the hospital as if they won the war. Don't you know these Hungarians were no better than the SS? In fact, some were more brutal."

The American was a bit taken aback, but that was it. So I returned in a few days and took my brother out. I brought him back with me to a hospital near Feldafing.

There were many situations similar to those at the hospital in Kham. The elite of the Hungarian army had fled when the Russians advanced into Hungary. They ran away and some of them ended up in that hospital. It was probably only a day's drive from Budapest. The American occupiers tolerated their presence. Admiral Horthy, the Hungarian chief of state allied with Hitler, had wound up in the German resort city of Garmisch in the mountains south of Munich. That is where he died, several years after the war. Our enemies were still all over the place.

Horthy's story is one of the great paradoxes of the war. How could he have escaped justice? He had instituted anti-Jewish laws and regulations, even before the Germans did. This might be balanced by the fact that he argued with Hitler over the fate of the last Jews left in Budapest and thus was to some degree responsible for their not being sent to concentration camps. In any case, memories are short. And, as far as the Allies were concerned, there were more important war criminals who had to be dealt with after the war. At least Horthy did not set up concentration camps in Hungary. This was in contrast to the Croats and the Slovaks, who did. In a world infected with evil, perhaps Horthy was a small fry.

I did not know if I would find my brother in that hospital, and he did not know whether my father, Buroch, and I were still alive. But when we finally saw each other it was a meeting without emotion. We had no emotions left. We just found him there, bandaged and in bed, and he told me what had happened. He was still just a kid, a teenager. No one cared. Not a tear was shed. Our emotions had been wrung out of us. It would take a lot of time for our emotions to return.

We took him to the hospital in Tutzing, which was in a plush resort area along the Starnberger See just six kilometers south of the huge camp at Feldafing. The hospital had been used previously by the German military, but now it was for the DPs who needed hospitalization. There my brother had one or two operations that were only partly successful. Later he was taken to a large hospital in Munich where he had still another operation. He never completely recovered from his wound.

I found Mendel in the summer of 1945. At the end of August, I decided I would go back to Romania to see if I could find anyone else. We had aunts, uncles, and cousins. We assumed that the aunts and uncles were no longer alive, but we hoped that some of our younger cousins had survived. I really had no hopes of finding anyone, but there was another reason for my return. My father said that he had buried certain personal family possessions and told me where they were. "Maybe you can find something," he said.

Those were the reasons I went, not for the purpose of staying there. Five of us, including my friend Steinmetz, decided to go. Steinmetz had learned that his wife was living in Satu Mare in Romania. So he was going to find her. The rest of us wanted to see what was happening in what had been our part of the world. So we left Munich to begin our journey back to Viseu.

To Viseu and Back

In August 1945 our plan was to travel by train across the Czech border to Pilsen, then on to Bratislava, Budapest, and, eventually, into Romania. It was to be a round-trip journey of approximately fourteen hundred miles across still-turbulent Europe. Russian and American armies occupied the lands we were to cross—Germany, Czechoslovakia, Hungary, and Romania. The number of displaced persons on the continent was to reach the staggering total of sixty million. National boundaries were unsettled. Transportation was chaotic. Travel documentation, supposedly required, was all but nonexistent. Huge waves of people were on the move, and almost all were headed west. We were going east, and we did not know what we would find.

We always had to wait for the trains. The Western Allies were careful at this time not to allow any of the German trains they controlled to leave the Allied zones and go east, because they knew they would never get them back. This meant that when we reached a station on the German side of the Czech border, we had to wait for a military train that could cross over. We had no passports, no documentation, no food, no suitcases, nothing. But we didn't worry. All we needed was a train headed in the right direction.

Near the border station we went into a bakery to get some bread. We had no ration cards. Why did we need them? we asked ourselves. "Ration cards are for you Germans," we said to the bakers, "not for us." We got the bread we wanted.

In the bakery, one of us noticed there were two suitcases standing alone on the floor. One of us said, "Those suitcases do not belong here. They need to be organized."

So I took one suitcase and one of the other men in our group took the other, and we went back to the station. There we opened the suitcases and said, "My G-d, we have found gold!"

One suitcase was loaded with cartons of cigarettes. The other was filled with bottles of all kinds of liquors. It was the greatest wealth anyone could find. As Martin Gilbert explained,

> No article of barter was so highly prized as the cigarette. Indeed, before long, the cigarette had . . . become the basic unit of exchange. . . . In reality, cigarettes were rarely smoked by the first person to obtain them, but were passed from person to person for profit or barter, changing hands a hundred times or more before reaching the end of the line—the smoker. Within a short while of the end of the war, Germany had become a civilization based on nicotine. The fate of the nation was enmeshed with the names of Lucky Strike and Camel.

We were happy because we now had currency that was really currency. Somebody apparently had just left the suitcases in the bakery. So we took them. Those cigarettes were to carry us for many months. We split them up, with each of us taking a few cartons. We were able to live on them until we got back to Germany from Romania. We also had enough whiskey to live on by bartering. It was a miraculous find.

We finally got a train and went on to Prague, where we saw the Russians throwing out the Germans who remained in the Sudetenland. They were sending them to Germany. From Prague the Russian-controlled trains were going southeast to the city of Brno. From Brno tracks led to the Soviet Union. In Prague we never went into the station. We stayed on the train, which remained on one of the freight sidings along with many other trains.

The Russians were taking home everything—furniture, carpeting, livestock, anything they wanted. The trains were loaded to the ceilings, and all were going to Russia. We soon learned that we had made a mistake. We had the wrong information about the train that we were on. Suddenly we noticed that it was heading due east. (We even had a compass with us just to make sure that we were not traveling in

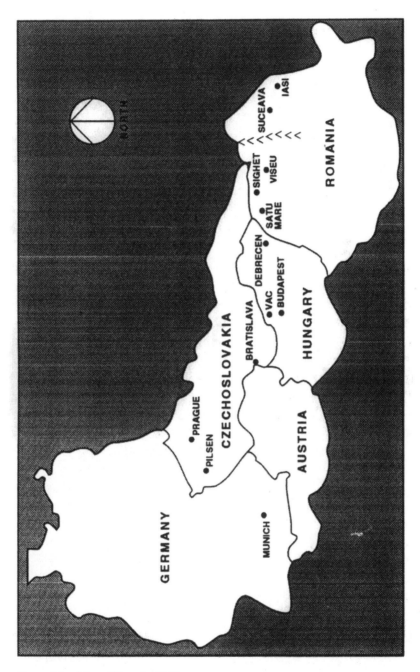

From Munich to Viseu in 1945.

the wrong direction.) Quickly we asked where the train was going. The answer was Russia. The train was going there, but we were not. We jumped off and hitchhiked back to the station, where we waited for the next train.

Czechoslovakia was not yet occupied by the Soviets. It was left alone. It was an anti-Nazi country and, in our minds, there was no border. We could go wherever we wanted to go, period. The new national borders had not yet been established. The Allies were moving forces from one country to another, from one zone of occupation to another one. At the Prague station we took an overnight train to Bratislava. We traveled, all the while aware that we had become very rich. When we arrived in Bratislava, we learned that there was a Jewish community center and that Jews had created various self-help organizations. These included communal housing and kitchens. The money to support them came from the American JOINT Distribution Committee, which had been formed in the First World War by American Jewish leaders to help Jewish refugees.

JOINT operations were all over that part of Europe. We found them in many cities and even in small Romanian towns where you might never expect them. In Bratislava we went to the JOINT center. We took showers, got cleaned up, and continued feeling very rich.

The next train would be to Budapest, which was only a couple of hours away. To make sure we didn't miss it, we went to the station early. It was August, and it was warm. A train pulled in from Budapest, and I heard a familiar voice. A woman on the train station platform was calling out a name, "Sacher, Sacher, Sacher." I followed the voice and saw that it was a cousin of mine doing the calling. Her brother was coming from Romania to meet her in Bratislava so they could go to Prague together and then on to the Sudetenland, where family members were.

The trains that came into that station were packed with thousands of people. My cousin arriving from Romania had just been married. He and his bride were among the thousands. Suddenly I saw him, and I screamed, "Hey, Sacher." We had not seen each other in who knows how long. He had been at the Russian front.

Sacher was an organizer and was able to do quite well for himself. I could see through the crowd that he had met his sister. I moved toward them. My cousins did not recognize me. I was wearing an American army jacket and pants. That was my way of traveling. People might very well have thought that I was a soldier. It was one of the techniques we used. I also wore a leather belt but had no gun. Nevertheless, I looked official. I had gotten taller and gained weight, and they had not seen me for three or four years. I had to tell them who I was. They then recognized my voice.

"Where are you going?" Sacher asked, and I told him to my town in Romania. "No," he said, "you are not going there."

"Why not?" I asked. "Because," he said, "you are coming with us. We are going to Leitmeritz" (a small town in the Sudetenland part of Czechoslovakia). "Our brothers and sisters and cousins are there. You come with us."

"I can't," I said. "I have my friends with me."

"Don't worry about friends," Sacher said. "Just come with us." So right there I had a meeting with my friends. I told them the situation, and they said for me to go. We could meet later in Satu Mare. After all, what was the rush? None of us had any work to do or any place to go.

But what were we going to do with our newly acquired wealth? We decided to split it. I took some of the cigarettes and they took some. We split them five ways. Then my cousins pulled me through a train window and, sure enough, I went back with them. It all happened completely by accident. I just recognized my cousin's voice and followed it. Incidentally, while I was dressed in a vaguely American uniform, both of my cousins were dressed in Russian uniforms. That was the technique. People thought you were someone important if you were in uniform. It gave more authority.

There were no tickets for those trains, and they were so jammed with passengers that you had to stand anywhere you could—on steps, the roof, anywhere. After I was pulled through the window, there was an overnight trip back to Prague and then to Leitmeritz. There I saw two more of Sacher's sisters and another one of my cousins. They were all on my mother's side—Rosenfelds. None of their parents had survived, but they survived there in the Sudetenland. There also were some people in Leitmeritz who were from our town.

I was there a few days. One of my cousins was my age, and she was leaving for Bratislava. From there she was going to travel to her hometown, which had been in Czechoslovakia but now had become part of the Soviet Union. It was in Ruthenia, which today is part of Ukraine. Thus the two of us embarked for Bratislava.

I had been in Bratislava for a few days when I heard that another cousin lived there. She had a fiancé who was an officer in the all-Jewish Czech brigade that was attached to the British army. (There also was a Jewish brigade composed of the men of Hungarian labor battalions who had been captured by the Russians. Many in the Czech brigade were Jews who had migrated to Palestine and volunteered in 1944. One of the cousins, whom I had met in Leitmeritz, had emigrated to Palestine in the 1930s and later volunteered for the Czech unit. He was an officer stationed in Leitmeritz until he was discharged.) I visited with my cousin in Bratislava for a few days and then moved on.

My discovery of more relatives along the route continued. I found that my cousin in Bratislava had a brother who survived the war in Budapest. He had not been taken to a concentration camp because he had been hidden and passed as a gentile. I stayed with him for a day. He originally had been from Sighet and asked if I would go to his house there, find clothes he had left, and bring them to Budapest when I came back. I agreed.

Then I went on to Satu Mare, where I caught up with my friends. Steinmetz had found his wife. He also found his sister. I told him I had returned to his wife's hometown, so now he had to go to mine. Together we headed for Viseu. There still was almost no public transportation in Romania. From Satu Mare to Sighet was about a four- or five-hour ride. There was a bus that traveled there, but it went only once a day and was loaded. It took us a while to buy our way on with cigarettes. Satu Mare had a communal kitchen where we ate, and Sighet, the next city of some size, had another. From Sighet to Viseu there were no buses, only a truck that went every few days.

In Sighet there were quite a few Jews. They were originally from the surrounding area but did not want to return to their villages. They were all young—there were no old people. Some of the young had come from concentration camps or from Hungarian work battalions on the Russian front. Many young people who had been in work battalions wound up as prisoners of war in Russia. The Russians viewed none of them as Jews. If you had been forced into a Hungarian work battalion, in the eyes of the Russians you were Hungarian.

There were instances, however, when Jewish officers in the Soviet army understood the difference and let the prisoners go. On other occasions, the Russians simply said, "You are wearing a Hungarian cap, therefore you are a Hungarian." Then they took them away to Russia. Some were later released. Others were kept for years. Most of the time no distinctions were made.

We hitchhiked from Sighet to Viseu in a truck. When I arrived, I did not go directly to the house where I had lived. The highway went directly into the center of town, so that is where I went. It had all been burned down. The Germans, when they retreated before the attacking Russians, had set fire to the entire main street. Most of the buildings were completely destroyed. They were cinders.

I arrived in the evening with Steinmetz. The others stayed in Satu Mare because they had found family members there. Steinmetz left his wife behind, and only the two of us came to Viseu. We got off the truck and looked for a communal house where we could eat and sleep, and found what there was. But Viseu was a ghost town. There were twenty, maybe thirty Jews where there had been almost five thousand just fifteen months earlier. That was it.

Only two Jews had remained behind, and they survived by hiding in the woods. They were older men in their thirties. One was my close friend, Wolf Genuth. He hid with another man, one who had always been successful avoiding the draft. Wolf was very smart and very cunning. After the ghetto was emptied and the Germans had left, he came into town with the other man—his name was Herrer. They took two Torah scrolls from the main synagogue, went back to the woods, and hid. Only a few days later the town was taken by the Russians. But it was already destroyed. The two men were the only ones who lived through all of that. In 1944, 4,269 people were sent to Auschwitz from Viseu. About forty survived.

Very few Germans were still there. I do not know how many. But there were no Hungarians that I knew of, and very few Jews. We ate in the communal kitchen and slept in a house that belonged to someone. Almost every other house was empty. No stores were open for business, although it was now more than a year after the war had ended in that part of Europe. My uncle's store had been burned down because it was in the center of the business section. Only its skeleton stood.

When the ghetto was established in the center of Viseu and the Jews were forced to move there, we could not take from our houses anything except what we could carry in a suitcase or satchel. All of the furniture and almost all of our clothes, books, utensils, and other possessions had to be left behind. After we were taken away, the town's Germans and a few Hungarians and Romanians went into the houses that belonged to the Jews and ransacked them, taking whatever they wanted. They also occupied any house they wanted.

Quite surprisingly, those who ransacked the houses gathered all the books they found and placed them in one of the two main synagogues in the center of town. That particular synagogue became full of books, in some places from the floors to the ceilings. When I returned to Viseu in August of 1945, the books were still there, tens of thousands of them. On that trip, however, we were still in somewhat of a daze. Nobody was looking for books. We were looking for any family members who might have survived, and I was looking for the boxes that my father had buried. We had no thought of saving books, even though they might be of value.

What subsequently happened to those books I do not know, with one exception.

Years ago I was sitting in a hotel in Bne Braq in Israel when a young man came up to me and said that he had a book which he thought I might find interesting. He then showed me the first volume of a six-volume set of the Mishna, the predecessor to the Talmud.

The Mishna was created after the Temple in Jerusalem was destroyed by the Romans in the year A.D. 70. Every devout Jew has a set of these books, and everyone learns their contents. My father had a set, and in it were recorded the names of his children and their birth dates.

I looked at the volume the young man had brought to me. It was faded. In fact, the color was completely gone from one cover. "You can have it," he said. So I took it and thanked him. I knew it was my father's book from looking at its cover. How the book got to Israel thirty years after the war and how it made its way to me after all those years is a mystery. It is now my most valuable possession—it is the only thing saved from my old home. I still remember when I learned in that book with my father as a child.

After the war few Jewish survivors of the concentration camps came home to Viseu. I do not know how many did, but there were a few. Some stayed. Almost all, however, eventually left. Before their departure, though, maybe for a year or two, there were some who thought they might reestablish themselves. They tried to return to an ordinary way of life. It did not last for long.

The reason was simple. The few who returned were all youngsters. There were no old people alive to come home. Some of the young people went home hoping to find someone or something. Some went to get married. But they went home to what was soon to become a Communist country. The Soviet army occupied the entire region, but it took about a year for the Communists to dominate the country. When they did, they communized everything. This included taking away all opportunity for an individual to operate an independent business. Store-keeping and other entrepreneurial activities were eliminated. This was done gradually, but the trend was clear.

The Jews who had gone back were capitalistic. They were small capitalists, not big ones. They were entrepreneurial and they could see that opportunities were not there. So, gradually, beginning in 1946, they started to leave Romania. In 1947 and 1948, they left en masse.

When I returned in 1945, there was a man in Viseu named Knohl. He had been at Dachau and the other camps with us. Even before the war he had been a Communist and had been imprisoned by the Hungarians. He was much older than I, and was constantly preaching that the Communists were the salvation of the world.

He was not from our town originally, but had married a woman from Viseu who came from a wealthy family. Nevertheless, he was a dedicated Communist. There were few of them in our town.

Knohl had suffered a lot in the camps and had barely made it through the war. He took a long time to recuperate afterwards. He was close to my father and had attempted to convince him of the virtues of Communism, how things would be under the Communists. Religion, Knohl said, was not going to mean anything. He was a dedicated atheist and was anti-religion, a typical dogmatic Communist.

After he recuperated, he returned right away to Romania. Almost as soon as he crossed the border, he became one of the leaders of the Communist movement. It was a time when people who wanted to could take almost anything. In Knohl's case he took the bus on which he had traveled back to Viseu and turned it over to the Communist Party. It was his gift, he said. Soon after his arrival home, he became the Communist czar for both our town and the immediate surrounding area.

When I came home in 1945, it was obvious to me that the Communists had taken care of themselves quite well. They took over the nicest houses in town. One of them was a house facing a garden that belonged to one of my aunts. She lived in the center of town where every house had a garden. In the back of her house there were several fruit trees. One of them was a plum tree. When I was visiting there late in August, the fruit was ripe. So I went to pick some. But I was being watched.

Knohl was occupying a house that faced my aunt's garden, and he saw me from one of the windows.

"What are you doing?" he called out.

"I'm picking the plums," I replied.

"You can't do that," he said.

I said, "What do you mean? I don't understand."

"That does not belong to you," said the Communist.

"Yes," I said, "I know it doesn't belong to me. It belongs to my aunt."

"No, no, no," said Knohl, "you don't understand. They belong to the government."

"What are you talking about?" I asked. "This is my aunt's garden." And I proceeded to pick the plums and kept on picking them.

"Cut it out," Knohl shouted. "If you don't, I'll shoot you." With that he took out his gun.

He won. I stopped picking the plums.

That was typical behavior for Communists in power.

To be under Communist rule was quite different than hearing about what they planned to do. Gradually, they tried to annihilate all vestiges of religion. The few surviving Jews who had returned were very religious. Even for those who were not still practicing, it was impossible for them to discard their traditions.

A significant event happened shortly after I left Viseu to return to Munich. There was a nearby town, Borsa, that had more survivors than ours. More of their people came home, and they were celebrating the holiday of Simchat Torah. They had prepared food for the meal that was to follow the synagogue service. But because it was part of a religious ritual, the Communist czar and a few of his associates viewed the preparation of the food as anti-government and, therefore, unacceptable. They destroyed the entire house where the meal was going to take place. That destructiveness alerted the people. It woke them up. After that, virtually all of them left.

From 1947 to 1952, 97 percent of the surviving Romanian Jews went to Israel. Chances are that some of them brought those books that had been gathered in Viseu, including the one later given to me in Bne Braq.

Other books and ritual objects from the past keep turning up. An instance of this occurred just a few years ago in Romania. It involved the great Klausenburger Rabbi who was an inmate with us from Auschwitz until liberation. During that time we became very close.

Just before he was taken to Auschwitz, he took his ritual valuables, like candelabra, spice boxes, and synagogue pieces used for ornamentation, and gave them to one of his sons to be buried. Before he was taken to Auschwitz, the son placed a note in the box he was to bury, stating that the items in it belonged to his father. That was it. No one survived except the Rabbi. After he was liberated, he did not return to Cluj, his town. Instead he came to America, where he built major institutions. Later in Israel he built an entire settlement in Netanya.

A few years ago there was some construction work underway in Cluj. While digging, workers suddenly struck something. It was a large box containing various silver pieces—the Rabbi's box. At first the workers hid it, but then they started to worry about what might happen to them if it was discovered that they had the box.

The construction workers decided they had better take the contents of the box to the police. The police, of course, realized that the box and its contents were valuable. They turned them over to a museum.

Last year, a Jew from Israel went to visit Cluj, which has grown to be one of the largest cities in the country. It has several institutions of higher learning and is often described as the university city. The visitor went to see the museum and spotted the ritual items that had belonged to the Rabbi, along with the note naming him as the owner.

The Romanian officials had known that the Rabbi was alive because he was very prominent. The visitor returned to Israel and talked about what he had found. By this time the Rabbi had been very sick for several years. But the information about the visitor's find was relayed to some of the Rabbi's followers, who contacted the Romanian government asking that the former possessions be returned. The government contended that the items were now part of that country's patrimony and could not be returned. But a deal was made. The officials were bribed, and a "loan" of the items was made. A "loan" that did not require to be repaid. (As I write this, the officials now say they want the items returned. "Negotiations" are underway. The items remain in Israel at present.)

The world is full of mysterious recoveries. A half century later, the Rabbi's valuable silver is found in a museum, and decades later the first volume of the Mishna belonging to my father is returned to me in a hotel in Israel.

The day after I arrived in Viseu, I went to explore our house to look for what my father had buried. There had been two boxes, one buried under the chicken coop and one under a storage room. The one under the storage room had been unearthed and stolen. The one under the chicken coop I found intact. It contained some of my mother's jewelry and some valuable pieces of her clothing. I also found two beautiful bedspreads, very fancy ones. They were my mother's heirlooms, things that one keeps forever. The valuable pieces of clothing consisted of my mother's shawl, an apron, and a kerchief she wore on Friday nights when she lit candles.

I had a cousin who at that time had been living in Iasi, Romania's second-largest city. She was an entrepreneurial woman, very resourceful. Her husband was a cousin of Ana Pauker who, after the war, was the chairman of the country's Communist Party. My cousin had not been in our town since the Hungarians occupied it in 1940. In 1944 her three sisters were seized and eventually taken to Bergen-Belsen. From there, after they were liberated, they went to Sweden. After the war, my cousin came to Viseu to see if any of her relatives were there. She was much older than I, a married woman with children, and someone who spoke very well. She was able to deal with Romanian authorities. She went to the chief of the gendarmes, told him she had heard that a box had been dug up at our house, and asked what had happened to it. The gendarmes gave all kinds of excuses. She said she had been trying to find the box but had been unable to do so.

We never got it back. The gendarmes had stolen it. That was their way of doing things.

Meanwhile, I found some hidden jewelry that belonged to my mother and my aunts. It had been hidden in the attic of my Uncle Buroch's house in what became our ghetto. There I also found a fifty-dollar bill that one of my uncles had sent from America. I was now very, very rich. I still had cigarettes and whiskey, and now money as well.

When I found this jewelry, my cousin, whose married name was Hannah Pauker, was still in town. I left the jewels with her temporarily, intending, of course, to take them back to my father when I left. I had been in Viseu for Rosh Hashanah and left the jewelry with her just a few days before Yom Kippur. On Yom Kippur Eve she disappeared. I looked for her all over the town, but she and the jewelry were gone. I knew, however, where she would go. So a friend and I embarked on a journey over the Carpathian Mountains to her home city of Iasi. I took some of the money I had found in the attic, along with some of the cigarettes, and hired a horse-drawn cart to take us across those high mountains.

The foothills began just two towns away, and then came the high elevations. It took us four or five days just to reach Suceava, which is the first town on the east side of the Carpathians and the place from where trains ran to Iasi. Unfortunately, the cart, with us in it, was too heavy for the horse to pull uphill, so we had to get out and walk. Downhill we couldn't ride in it either, because it went so fast that it was likely to roll over. So we walked alongside the horse most of the way. There was almost no level ground on the trip. From Suceava we caught a train going farther east.

For our passport we had an ingenious document we had obtained back in Sighet. The people at the communal center there had devised a document in three languages—Russian, English, and Romanian. The stamp that was on it did not mean anything, but it looked very official. So we used it on this portion of the trip as our passport. Consequently, we had no passport problem with the Romanians. At the same time I continued to wear my uniform.

We showed the "passport" to the conductor and it was perfect. But he said we still needed tickets. I asked what kind of tickets. As far as I knew, I said, no tickets were needed.

"That's not what I mean," said the conductor. "I mean I've got to get my—" Before he finished, I gave him a couple of cigarettes. They were the tickets.

On the way back I bought a real ticket, got on the train, and the same conductor said, "Why did you go and buy a ticket? I'll let you ride cheaper than with a ticket." We had bought tickets but still had to pay off the conductor.

When I found Hannah Pauker in Iasi, she had all kinds of stories. "I had to do this," and "I had to do that," and "I had to bribe someone." But the jewelry was gone and we never got it back, never.

My cousin is alive in Israel, but I never talk to her. Through the years she wrote to my father and the rest of us a dozen times. My wife, however, is the only one to whom I have told this story. My cousin wanted to come to America and had other family intervene in trying to reach me and my father, but we have always refused to meet her. She had our cousins beg us many times.

We made another difficult trip back over the Carpathian Mountains to Viseu, then traveled back to Sighet and Satu Mare. Again we had to go by bus. From Satu Mare the bus went through the town of Valea de Mihai on the way to the border with Hungary. The first major town in Hungary was Debrecen.

While I was in Viseu, the Russians had formalized the borders of the countries they occupied, so I could not return the same route I had come. Again I was traveling with Steinmetz, but this time also with his wife and sister, whom we picked up in Satu Mare. There were others as well, I don't know how many, but there were more of us going back to Munich than had started out. The fifty dollars I had found in my uncle's attic was still helping. It carried me the entire time I was in Romania. The reason was that the value of the dollar kept going up. Inflation was atrocious and, as a result, the exchange rate kept doubling every few days. So I kept changing the money I had into smaller bills and sold enough dollars to keep us going. Actually, the fifty dollars carried me and my friends all the way back to Germany.

Our round trip took a total of about six weeks. It was much more difficult than I anticipated.

The Russians were now vigorously imposing their border regulations. Massive numbers of people were trying to run away from the areas the Soviet army had occupied. The highways heading west were jammed with every possible mode of transportation—carts drawn by horses and oxen, people walking—and everything that could move was loaded to maximum capacity. People were paying whatever they had to escape the Russians, especially Jews trying to reach the British and American zones. Their hope was that from there they would be able to get to Palestine faster.

Meanwhile, Romania was attempting to impose Communism on its people. At the end of 1944, with the advance of Soviet troops, Romania had turned its coat and joined the Allies. Then, in 1945, the Communists began consolidating their power. Bercu Feldman became the so-called Jewish czar to eliminate any semblance of religion among the Jews. He had been a religious Jew but now sought to eradicate religion. The people were aware of this, and many of those who had been Communists were disenchanted. They started to pick themselves up and leave. You could see it happening in towns all over the country.

But ahead of us now was the border with Hungary, and Hungary was in turmoil. The Russians were there, setting up a Communist government, but it was not even as orderly as the one in Romania. When we got to the border, there were no trains. Nothing was scheduled to leave for days, maybe weeks. What were we going to do? Then suddenly we saw a steam engine arriving. Its engineer was a Hungarian. We told him that we were trying to get back to Munich. When he heard that, his price went up. We offered him a cigarette and he said OK. We could ride on the coal tender. There was room, he said.

But there was a slight problem. The train had no coal. We looked around and eventually found a pile of it. We told the guy who was in charge of the coal that we wanted some, but he said we couldn't have it. Then we offered him a cigarette and he, too, said OK. We helped the engineer shovel the coal. It was very hot. I began to wonder why we should be forced to ride on a coal tender. We had the two women with us, and there were all sorts of other people grabbing at anything to get on the coal tender. We would have to do better than that.

We decided we wanted to have an entire railroad car to ourselves. We figured that we had been able to get the coal, so we ought to be able to buy a passenger car. We located the same guy who had sold us the coal and told him we wanted a car attached to the coal tender. He said no problem. For a few more cigarettes, we got a railroad car. Before we knew it, the car was full of people. They were there as soon as the door was opened, and they did not ask if they could get in. You couldn't push them away. So the car quickly filled.

Then, suddenly, some Russian officers appeared and asked us where we were going. To Budapest, we said. The Russians wanted to go there too, but they said there didn't seem to be enough room. No problem, we said. We got more cars attached. Within a short time we had an entire train.

We started moving westward. At every stop more people jammed onto the train. At Debrecen we had to "buy" another train in order to continue on to Budapest. By the time we reached Szolnok, deep in Hungary, our train was filled to the limit of every car. People wanted to get to Budapest because they would have a better chance of escaping from the Soviets if they could get there.

Then another train arrived from a Russian-occupied area. The people on it were screaming and jumping off when they saw our train headed for Budapest. They crowded in, jamming our train even more. We met some Jewish girls who were terribly afraid of the Russian soldiers. We helped them get onto our train.

At that time we were in a passenger car. It was night and very dark. Suddenly we heard some commotion. The Russian officers and soldiers, who were traveling with us, were robbing everyone. They took whatever they could get their hands on. They took everyone's valuables, even suitcases. For some reason they didn't rob us. But in the morning we learned that they had robbed everybody else at gunpoint.

As we came nearer to Budapest, we went through a rich farm area. The last few cars of the train were flatbeds, and many of the local women climbed aboard with animals and produce they wanted to sell in the Budapest market. With them they had chickens, ducks, geese, and even livestock. As a result of all the pushing and shoving, many people fell from the train and were killed under its wheels.

When we arrived in Budapest, I went to see my cousin, Tuli, who had asked me to try to find a coat he had left in Sighet. I had found it and gave it to him, although it was a bit torn. We stayed in Budapest a couple of days and then headed north toward Bratislava. The first town on the way was Vac. A short distance north of it was the Czechoslovakian border, which by then was in place. You needed passports to cross.

We got off the train in Vac and walked around. It was a beautiful town. We asked if there were any Jewish places, but learned that the people there were very anti-Semitic and that all the local Jews had been killed. "There are no more Jews," they said. "Get out of here. Don't come here. There are no more Jews here. Don't ask us questions. They are all dead."

In the middle of the night we resumed our journey north again on the train toward Bratislava and crossed the Czech border. Again Russians went from car to car robbing everybody of everything. I had with me the few precious things that had belonged to my mother. "Give them to me," said a Russian. I said I couldn't. "They were my mother's."

"You don't understand," said the Russian. "This is a gun and I will shoot you."

I said, "Please don't take them," but they took away everything except the apron my mother wore, the kerchief, and the beautiful shawl.

The Russian soldiers robbed everyone all the time. In Sighet I had seen Russian soldiers start at the opposite ends of a street and go from house to house, robbing everyone. They were mainly after watches and went down that street putting as many as they could on their arms.

In Bratislava there was another check of our passports. Again the "Sighet passport" worked, and we went on to Prague. This was a regularly scheduled train and, again, it was packed. More Czech conductors came aboard. So I took out my "Sighet passport." "Wait a minute," one of the conductors said. "This might be a passport but you still have to pay for a ticket." I told them I had no money. We were in concentration camps, I said, and were returning to Germany. After negotiations back and forth, they said to go ahead. I think by that time I didn't have any more cigarettes, just a few dollars. It did not matter with the Czechs because they could not be bribed. They were always very friendly to Jewish refugees, and very hostile toward Germans and Hungarians.

Then we came to an area north of Karlsbad. It was the beginning of the American-occupied zone. The train stopped. Nobody was to cross into that zone. The Third Army was in place. They knew that many people from Eastern Europe were seeking to enter the American zone. At that time the zone included a portion of Czechoslovakia, and the train which we were on could not enter with anyone other than people living in those areas.

An American soldier told us firmly that we were going nowhere. We were taken off the train and had to make our way back to Karlsbad. There were six or seven of us traveling together. In Karlsbad we found another Jewish communal home. The city had become a principal center for people coming from the east seeking to enter the American zone. We met people in the communal house who had fled from Poland, Russia, and Ukraine. They either had been in hiding from the Germans or were in work battalions on the eastern front. Technically only those persons who were liberated in the four occupied zones were considered to be displaced persons. The others did not have the same privileges. In fact, they did not receive any help from the United Nations Relief and Rehabilitation Administration until maybe ten months after the war. For a long time anyone who did not have a DP card was not entitled to any rations. After a while, however, that didn't mean much because you received nothing and had to make your own way.

Even though I was a displaced person, I had left the American-occupied zone. Once you did that and returned to your hometown, you lost your displaced person status.

From Karlsbad, we had to figure out how to make our way back to Munich. We found a Russian soldier, a Jew, who knew the area. He had maps and told us not to worry. We would make it. Using his maps, we crossed over into the American zone on foot. It was a mountainous area, very beautiful and rugged. The women with us struggled, but we managed to get to the nearest town in the American zone where a train stopped. Sure enough, we got on a train and nobody stopped us.

Next we arrived in Pilsen. It is a large city, but trains did not run west from there into Germany as frequently as they did into other parts of Czechoslovakia. Pilsen was inundated with Germans who were going back to Germany after having been chased out of the Sudetenland. We had to wait for a train because hundreds of thousands of those Germans were being evacuated. In fact, in Leitmeritz, where my cousins were now living, any house of a German that a Jew wanted was free for the asking. The Allies agreed to remove all Germans from the allied countries of Czechoslovakia, Poland, and Yugoslavia. Many millions were moved.

For some unaccountable reason, the Americans were allowing those Germans to enter the zone at the same time they were barring all those people who had been hiding from the Germans or serving in work battalions. There were many things that did not make sense. But the evacuation of the Germans from the rest of Europe was one of the deals that had been made among the Allies at Yalta. Stalin made it part of the deal that forced all the Russian war prisoners to go back even if they didn't want to. There were many grim ironies like that.

The German evacuation was well organized. When they entered

the American zone, all the schools and other public facilities were turned over to them as places to sleep. There were a lot of German refugees, but they were not fleeing like desperate people. They were calm and self-assured.

In Pilsen we still had to figure out a way to get back to Germany. Again we found a Jewish communal house. The town itself was reasonably well governed and tranquil. The Germans there had lots of marks, which they were exchanging at almost no value for dollars or other currency. The mark had no value in Pilsen but would have when brought into Germany. So I bought whatever I could. I had a sizable amount of them in a pouch around my waist. We all did. We bought them cheap.

Eventually we got on a train headed for the German-Czech border. When we got there, a Czech guard asked us if we had any money or anything else that we should declare. We said no, nothing. But he searched us. That was the end of our money. He took it away. He caught us. We didn't complain. We just continued on our way back to Germany.

It still took a while for us to reach Munich. We went through Kham, which was where I had found my brother Mendel, and then we traveled through much of Bavaria. When we finally made our way to Munich, I told my father and my brothers that I had found almost nothing, just the few belongings of our mother, and some of them had been taken from me by the Russians at gunpoint. All that remained were her apron, her shawl, and her kerchief. That was it.

Restless

It was October of 1945 when I arrived back in Munich. After I gave an account of my journey to my father and my two brothers, we tried to make sense of what we were going to do.

Mendel was still in a hospital. My father, Buroch, and I took over another apartment. At that time we had two or three of them. My father's health was much better. The three of us were literally inundated with people coming into Munich and the American zone from Romania, Hungary, and other parts of Eastern Europe. Our barracks and apartments were very busy places. The refugees from the East received food from us and slept in our quarters, but they all wanted to move on. No one wanted to stay. They wanted to go to Palestine. Their immediate objective was to find a way to get to the nearest port. At a port they at least had a chance of departing for the Middle East. Marseilles was one of the favorite objectives. Genoa was another.

As the winter began to set in, conditions for the German people became very bad. There were shortages of food and just about everything else. The apartments grew colder. So we started some entrepreneurial efforts. The Americans called it the "black market," but we called ourselves entrepreneurs. We tried all kinds of things to make a few bucks. Most of the time we succeeded. We bought low and sold high. It was basically bartering. We simply had become businessmen, meeting the demands of our customers.

My friend Steinmetz, who now had his wife, his sister, and his wife's sister with him, took over what I can only describe as a gigantic apartment. It had been occupied by a dentist, so they were in the high-rent district. In fact, their next-door neighbor was the chief of police in Munich, an older gentleman. That is, he was older than Buroch, Steinmetz, my other friends, and I, and anyone who was older than us was old. Steinmetz's apartment was very close to us, and it became a meeting place for many of the Jewish leaders coming to Munich.

We became friendly with the chief of police, and he constantly asked us about the possibility of getting some food and other supplies he wanted. No problem, we said. Here is the deal, we told him. We will give you all of the food and whatever else you need. All we want from you are two things. One is an official police stamp. The other is blank travel documents.

He agreed to give us these, and we had a deal—that is how I became the official creator of documents to travel from Munich to France. It was quite informal, but then nothing at that time was formal. There was no such thing as a passport for all the DPs.

The chief had probably been a Nazi. He could not have been chief of police without having been one. He obviously talked himself out of that past because he remained chief under the U.S. occupation. Actually, he was a nice guy.

People came to us who wanted to go elsewhere. "Where do you want to go?" I asked them. "Do you want to go to France? OK." I created the document to authorize so and so to go, stamped it, and they went to France. It did not matter that the Munich police had no authority to allow people to cross a national border. What I was giving out was an "official" document, or at least an official-looking one, and it was given to any person who wanted to travel. At that time everything was chaotic, including the borders. We began sending people to Paris if they wanted to go there. Almost everybody wanted to get out of Germany as fast as possible. The only ones who wanted to stay were those who were too sick to leave, or people who had shown they had no moral fiber, like the capos who sold out to the Germans in the camps. Germany, with its people, was not where survivors wanted to reestablish themselves.

Some of those who wanted to leave, however, soon grew disenchanted because they could not go to Palestine. There were so many obstacles against getting there and life there was so hard, but people still wanted to go. Despite all the hardships, thousands and thousands did go.

The war had been over now for more than five months, and a mass influx of people began arriving in Munich from Poland and Russia. In 1939 and 1940, when the eastern half of Poland had been occupied by Russia, many Jews fled from the German-controlled portion to the Russian side. When Hitler invaded the Soviet Union on June 22, 1941, those Jews were either voluntarily or forcibly moved away from the front lines deeper into Russia. Many thousands were moved toward the Turkish border, where they lived in very primitive conditions and had to fend for themselves. But there were no concentration camps for them, no forced labor. They were on their own. The communal life continued.

When the war ended, the Russian and Polish governments allowed those Jews to go back to Poland. (Many Russian Jews claimed to be Polish in order to escape from Russia.) They had no knowledge of crematoria, no knowledge of Auschwitz. They did not know what had happened. They came home and found devastation. Most started immediately to move west into Germany because, to them, that meant being in the American zone. Those who were unable to enter the American zone went to the British one.

In many Polish towns after the war, Jews who returned were killed by Poles. During the German occupation, when Jews were taken to concentration camps, Poles had taken over their homes. They did not want to give back those stolen properties. After the killings started, the Jews who had come home left immediately. On the way they passed through Czechoslovakia, a very friendly country. When the war ended, Czechoslovakia quickly reestablished its government. It was democratic and had very good people. They allowed Jewish refugees to come. Some settled in homes vacated by Germans. But most used the country as a thoroughfare on the way to Germany. They came to Munich because it was on the natural path. It became the site of the first and largest concentration of DPs.

A Jewish communal center was established there with the help of the American JOINT Distribution Committee. Again, the goal of those Jews coming from Russia and Poland was Palestine. If they could not go there, the goal was America. To reach either objective, they wanted to get to the American zone or, if that wasn't possible, the British zone.

Shortly after I came back from Viseu, I decided I wanted to enroll in the university in Munich to study textiles. However, I did not have a sufficient education in mathematics. So I hired a teacher to help me prepare. Any Jew could now get into the university immediately without any questions being asked. There were no quotas; there were no lines. Jews were accepted. But not many enrolled. I was one of the few. I began going to the university off and on. It was not yet really organized. Classes were not frequent. The classrooms had no heat and were quite cold. Teachers were not always available.

Meanwhile, we had to make a living. We were buying, selling, and bartering. With all the refugees, Munich had become a vast marketplace. The market was established at the Mohlstrasse, which was where the JOINT office and various agencies dealing with DPs were located. The Americans called it a black market, but it was just a plain market. You bought and you sold. Nothing was legal because you had to have a ration card for everything. The American MPs frequently raided the marketplace and confiscated the wares and foreign currencies.

I don't remember how we got our supplies, but it didn't matter. The supplies and rations that we got did not amount to much, because the German mark had no value. The currency was in dollars and the gold coins of many countries. There was also the scrip that the military used.

You bought different things from the GIs, valuable items like cigarettes, tobacco, chocolate, ladies' hosiery—anything. After a while we grew so rapidly that we became a big business. We had to take more apartments. By this time we had three or four of them away from the camp.

We were living in the Funk Kasserne camp; in addition to the apartments we controlled, we had our own barracks in the camp. Funk Kasserne held many thousands of people. It also was the main distribution center for all United Nations Relief and Rehabilitation

Administration supplies in the region. An endless number of trains kept coming with food and other necessities to be unloaded for distribution. We were able to get three of our people to work in the UNRRA warehouse in order to buy supplies for us to sell. They were two sisters and a brother by the name of Birnbaum from a town near our own in Romania.

We developed a sophisticated "traffic pattern." Czech soldiers came and bought stuff from us in German marks. They had purchased the marks in Czechoslovakia at a cheaper rate from Germans who were fleeing west. We bought the marks from the Czechs for cheap and sold them stuff that we got from the UNRRA warehouse. We had a conglomerate. We received their orders of what they would need on their next visit during the following week. It was well organized. In the apartments we controlled we could do business with several hundred people at one time. It was busy.

At Christmas time, UNRRA brought in all kinds of items to be distributed. We decided that it was an opportune time to do some extra business. Giant boxes of merchandise had been brought into the warehouse. We asked ourselves, "Why do we have to take that stuff piecemeal? We'll take it in those large crates." The UNRRA people were busy with Christmas preparations. This was a great opportunity for us, and we took advantage of it.

So stuff started coming to us by the box, and we were loaded to the rafters. We had shirts, underwear, cigarettes—tons and tons of stuff. Every week the Czech soldiers would come and buy what we had. On one occasion we even sold them a truck we had obtained so they could haul their stuff away.

Then on Christmas Eve 1945 there was pandemonium. I was not in the barracks at the time. I was out transporting a load of stuff, but my father, Buroch, and the rest of the gang were there. In one of the other barracks there was a celebration. During the course of it a U.S. Army lieutenant was killed by one of the Slavs in a drunken fight. The result was a midnight raid on the barracks by the Americans. They went from barracks to barracks to find the killer. Instead they found all that contraband. They took everything away. They also took my father, my brother, and all of our visitors to jail.

The barracks were not only a place where we kept stuff. Many other people whom we knew used it as their own storage space. They had beds there, stayed as long as they wanted, and then went away, leaving their stuff behind. A week or two later, they would come back to get it. Their stuff was everywhere, under mattresses, everywhere. Some of the people had cloth for suits. Some had cigarettes. Some had money in all kinds of currencies and denominations. Some had gold—all kinds of things. Now, however, everything was gone.

The next morning, when I came back to the barracks, some of the men who were there asked me what I was doing. Didn't I know what had happened? Then they told me. "They are looking for you," one of the men said. "They know there was one missing and that you are the one. You better get out of here fast."

I got out fast, but not before I looked inside and saw that the place was in a shambles. The Americans had turned the place upside down. But under one mattress I found some gold coins. I took them and disappeared.

My father and brother were in jail for thirty days. Then they had a trial. They were sentenced to the time already served. But the Americans had taken everything away, and we had to start anew. We were all but wiped out. All I had were those gold coins. The question was, what do I do with them? I sold them and bought a piece of cloth for a suit.

In the meantime, the guy who owned the coins came back. He showed up, went to the barracks, and was looking for his gold. I asked him what he was looking for, and he said that he had something but now it was gone. Then he heard about the raid.

"Does that mean that everything is gone?" he asked.

"Yes," I said, "but they did not get your gold pieces."

"What do you mean?" he asked. So I told him the story.

"I found them and I sold them and I have the cloth. As soon as I sell the cloth, I will give you the money for your gold."

When I sold that piece of dark blue cloth for a suit, I made a nice profit and gave him back his original money. After that my father said we had to do things in a different way. We had to have a business that was legal. So he began running a kosher restaurant. Everyone who came from Poland, Romania, and other places in the East, and who either knew us or had met someone who told them about us, came for food.

Germany was a monopolistic country. The Lowenbrau brewery company, for example, owned many, many restaurants, and Lowenbrau was the only beer served at each. Before it was expropriated, Lowenbrau was owned by a Jew. I don't know who had the ownership at the end of the war but, somehow or other, we became aware of the availability of a particular Lowenbrau restaurant in Munich, and my father was able to buy it. We made it the first kosher restaurant in the city, and it became a very well-known place. We sold Lowenbrau beer, and anyone who wanted to be sure of a good meal came there. It was a gathering place. My father owned it until he came to America.

Meanwhile, we were restless. We tried to go to the United States, but the only way was to have an affidavit sent by someone there saying that he would support you if you were not able to support yourself. With that affidavit and by being part of the quota, you were able to go.

In the eyes of the U.S. government, my two brothers and I were Romanians, since that is where we were born. My father was Hungarian because he was born in Viseu when it was in Hungary. For each of those countries, the quota was about three hundred people a year. There were preferential admissions through members of Congress and for close family members—sons, daughters, husbands, wives, mothers, fathers. When those preferences were admitted, the numbers under the quotas were correspondingly lowered. As a result, being included in the Romanian and Hungarian quotas meant at least a ten-year wait. So having an affidavit did not amount to much. In fact, it didn't mean anything.

So to go to America as part of a quota was practically impossible. In the meantime, we tried to think of what we could do so that we could go. Our total focus was on getting out of Germany. All our activities revolved around that. This also was the preoccupation of everyone else. No one could stay in the land that had committed such atrocities against us and against our people.

On Yom Kippur, early in October of 1945, while I was still on my trip back from Viseu, General Eisenhower visited the Feldafing camp.

He had announced in advance that he was coming, and a special tent was put up for the services that he and thousands of others would attend. The only rabbi of stature who was there was Rabbi Halberstam, the Klausenburger Rabbi. He was now fairly healthy, and he performed the services. By that time his reputation was known by everyone, including the Americans, UNRRA, and others involved with camp welfare.

Eisenhower was welcomed like an emperor, with salt and bread and the usual rituals. He then asked the rabbi what he could do to help. The rabbi said the main need was for adequate living quarters. An average of eighteen to twenty people were living in each room in Feldafing, and the congestion was getting worse. More and more people kept coming from other countries. Eisenhower gave an order right there on the spot. The nearby town of Tutzing was to be vacated immediately. Nobody could take from there more than a suitcase. The Germans were required to turn over the entire town to Jews—the entire town. It was a town where many of the elite lived or had summer homes. It made no difference. They had twenty-four hours to get out. Many resented the order to evacuate, and some fought it. But an order was an order.

"What else do you want?" the general asked the rabbi. "I want to have a camp," the rabbi said, "where we can practice our religion." Again Eisenhower said all right. There was another camp, he said, that could be provided, and he gave the Jews the Fernwald camp a few miles away.

When Fernwald became the Jewish religious camp, all of a sudden everyone became religious. "I'm religious," people were saying, although some of them had not been saying that a minute earlier.

The rabbi was a very powerful individual. He was an impressive speaker and a great scholar. He was a stirring orator who spoke only in Yiddish. He entranced his listeners; when he spoke at communal events, he did so with his eyes closed. He knew the Torah and the commentaries by heart. He knew everything. He tried to give people hope, to build them up. To the many thousands of Jewish displaced persons, he said your families were religious, your forefathers were religious, and religion is going to be the only thing that will save you. Why we suffered for all these years, why we lost our families, is not for us to understand. It is G-d's will. We are not to question His motive. We have to accept it unquestioningly.

He drew many disciples, including my brother Buroch. Buroch had decided he did not want to engage in our businesses in Munich. He was one of the young people—he was seventeen in 1945—who were drawn to Rabbi Halberstam and his religious activities. Buroch would become very closely associated with the rabbi for the rest of the rabbi's life.

At the end of 1945, I began to look for other ventures. I traveled back and forth across Germany, mostly on business. This went on into 1946. Everyone was restless. We wanted to leave Germany, but we weren't able to do so. We assumed that we would not be able to go to America in the foreseeable future.

Aachen, a major German city, played a part in our business. Near the border with both Belgium and the Netherlands, it was the first city the Allies entered when they crossed into Germany. It had been almost totally wiped out.

Aachen had been a major textile manufacturing center, but now the factories were in ruins. In Aachen I saw the worst destruction of any place in Germany. I never saw Dresden, but of the cities I saw, Aachen was the worst. We went scrounging around and found an old lady who knew where there was still a sizable amount of cloth. She took us to see either the owner or the president of a factory that manufactured it. "It's gone," he told us. "There is no more here, but I know where you can get some." Through him we found plenty of cloth.

Düsseldorf and Cologne, located not far from each other along the Rhine River, were in the industrial heart of Germany. Products made there were being sought by our Czech customers in Munich. One product was needles for sewing machines. A number of other products were also in great demand in Czechoslovakia. We found out what was marketable there and what was salable in other countries in Eastern Europe.

In Düsseldorf, I came across a taxi driver who had been jailed as a Communist under Hitler and was very proud of it. We became friends. He became my chauffeur, more or less, and all it cost was a carton of cigarettes. He took me to places where I could find products

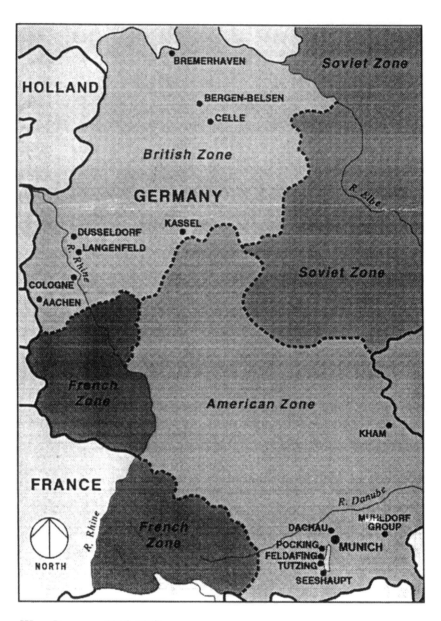

West Germany, 1945–1947.

sought by the Czechs. Then the goods were brought to Munich, where we sold them. They would be shipped to the East and sold there by others.

The Allies were opening more and more DP camps. There were maybe two dozen located near various cities in the British and American zones in both Germany and Austria. They were built in areas where there already was a nucleus of DPs, like Bergen-Belsen. In the Munich area there were Feldafing and Fernwald. Near Nuremberg there was the Furth camp. There also was a major camp near Frankfort.

The number of DPs and the number of camps continued to grow, mainly because of all the Poles coming back from Russia and those Russians who were able to get out by pretending that they were Poles. You were supposed to have a passport, but you could buy a piece of paper anywhere showing that you were born in whatever country you wanted—that you were born, for example, in Warsaw, and thus you were a Pole. You took a chance, but so what? Taking a chance was less onerous than not being able to get out. The DPs had no fear.

I made another trip to Bergen-Belsen to see what was going on there. By that time the camp had been cleaned up. It, too, had an influx of people, including many of those who had nowhere to stay in the Munich area.

Adjacent to the Bergen-Belsen DP camp the British established a huge camp for General Anders's Poles. They had fought alongside the Germans in North Africa until they were captured and allowed to serve with the British. They were former turncoats and very anti-Semitic, but the British protected them. They also had the protection of the Polish government in exile in London, and were supposed to be going back to Poland.

Bergen-Belsen had become a giant camp with many thousands of Jewish DPs. It had a complete infrastructure, with a camp president and all sorts of organizations. They arranged for many people from there to go to Palestine through Marseilles and other ports, including ones in Belgium. But the Poles in the other camp started to attack the Bergen-Belsen Jews, and there were a couple of killings. Then the Jews fought back and it stopped.

I became involved. I was near Bergen-Belsen almost every week because Düsseldorf and Cologne were not far from there. We also went occasionally to Hanover, Hamburg and other nearby cities to look for whatever we might want to buy. From Bergen-Belsen, I got the idea to start looking for ways to go to Palestine. Young Jews were being recruited at Bergen-Belsen and were secretly given military training, including the use of small arms. I became part of one of those groups. We got hold of a castle, an estate that had belonged to Franz von Papen, the former German ambassador to Turkey who had been one of the key men in the rise of Hitler to power.

At Von Papen's estate in Langenfeld, several hundred people were trained for the struggle in Palestine. The leaders were men from Britain's Jewish Brigade who came to conduct the training after they had been discharged in Italy at the end of the war. They were aided by Jews still on duty with the British army. They had to be careful to keep their commanders from knowing about such activity.

We had to be very careful that the British, in whose zone of occupation the estate was located, did not become aware of our activities, because they knew from experience that those combat-hardened Jewish soldiers were motivated to get as many trained DPs as possible to Palestine. They feared that the Jewish Brigade would be the nucleus of the armed force that would fight for the creation of a Jewish state—and they were right. In the confusion that prevailed after the war was over, and before new borders had been established, those doing the training were able to get into Germany, even though the British did everything they could to stop them. We had to be very, very careful. Fortunately Langenfeld was in a fairly isolated location midway between Cologne and Düsseldorf.

At the beginning of 1947, I decided I would go to Palestine. I was twenty years old. I would go to Palestine and become actively involved in the struggle to create the state of Israel. We were told that several hundred people from our military training group would be shipped out shortly. Our group was allotted a certain number of places. I was scheduled to go in the spring of 1947. The ship that was to take us to Palestine had been renamed the *Exodus*. It was to depart from

Rotterdam in the Netherlands. The plan of the organizers was for us to go out of Bergen-Belsen in ambulances. The British guards routinely allowed one or two DPs to leave camp without questioning. But if a larger number attempted to leave, the British asked questions about where they were going and why, especially if the group was leaving with their belongings.

For more than two hundred DPs to take off in ones and twos would take days. So we left in ambulances with maybe as many as twenty in each. It was arranged that the guards would be distracted at the moment of our departure, often by having girls talk to them. Even in those numbers it still took a while for all of us to reach the gathering point at a nearby farm. There we were told that trucks would pick us up to drive us across the border to Rotterdam.

At the appointed time the trucks arrived. We numbered several hundred, including Jewish Palestinians who had been part of the Jewish Brigade that fought alongside the British. They had been demobilized in Italy because the British knew if they reached Germany they would organize others to get to Palestine. Instead of going directly home to Palestine, the brigade members changed their IDs to become DPs and went to the displaced persons' camp in Germany. Their original identities were given to DPs who went to Palestine instead of them. They even gave the DPs their uniforms.

Their organization was called Bricha, which means "escape" in Hebrew. Everyone knew there was such an organization, but they did not know exactly where it was operating at any given time. Bricha had recruits all over the place ready to go to Palestine, especially in port cities. They would go to places where there were Jews to recruit and train. A couple of these men were with us when we left the farm.

Somehow, the trucks on which we were riding were delayed. We were scheduled to arrive at the German-Belgian border before eight o'clock at night, but we were late. The border was guarded by soldiers of the three allies, the United States, Britain, and France, on different shifts. The Americans were always friendly and sympathetic. The British were the opposite. As for the French, it depended on the situation. At eight o'clock there had been a change of shifts, and the British replaced the Americans as the guards. When we arrived, the British asked, "Where the hell are you guys going?" We answered that we were going to Cuba. "What the hell," said the guards. "Why are so many people going to Cuba? What's going on?"

They became very suspicious, and the whole thing blew up in our faces. We were held there for some days. A Jewish member of Parliament even flew over from London. Then the highest-ranking American officer tried to overrule the British. But rank, said the British, had nothing to do with the dispute, and nobody was going to tell them what to do. They were all arguing about whether we should be allowed to cross the border and go on to Rotterdam.

The mayor of Cologne at that time was a Jewish intellectual who had been in a concentration camp. He later became a member of Konrad Adenauer's government in the new Federal Republic of Germany. He came to the border crossing and tried to intercede on our behalf, but even he couldn't persuade the British to let us go.

During our detention, some of us got sick because it was bitterly cold for those of us stuck on the trucks. Finally, the people arguing on our behalf decided it was no use. The arrangements to get through were off. They gave up, and we were taken to Cologne in the middle of the night. We concluded that we would have to go back. "Go back where?" asked the mayor. "You're not supposed to exist. Remember, you never left Bergen-Belsen. Where are you going back to?"

So they put us up. We were taken to a public school in Cologne. The school was in session during the day, but we were put up at night. That first night none of us slept. Instead we roamed around the school. It was dark, but we walked around. Suddenly we saw crosses on the walls. All the public schools in Cologne had crosses. We said, "What is going on? We are supposed to be sleeping with crosses?" And some of us broke the crosses out of anger and frustration.

In the morning we had not yet left when the kids arrived and found the school in a shambles. There was pandemonium; it was a big scandal. The mayor came and he tried to pacify everybody. Our exodus from Germany had failed.

Later that day we were transported by trolley cars to a bunker in town. Every large city had bunkers, concrete buildings where the population went when there was an air raid. They were considered bombproof unless there was a direct hit. We were housed in one of those shelters, all two hundred of us. We were there for about a week.

During that period, men from the Jewish Brigade came and looked us over. They wanted to see which of us seemed to match the identification papers and photographs they had. These papers were to be used to get us out of the country and on to Palestine. The papers were used many times over. Unfortunately, I didn't match any of them. It didn't matter anyway. I had already decided that I was going to return to Munich. My father knew nothing about what I had been doing in Langenfeld, Bergen-Belsen, and Cologne.

I returned to Munich around May of 1947. I told my father the whole story and how I still wanted to go to America. Then, by word of mouth, we found out that there was an American Children's Committee that was going to take five hundred kids up to eighteen years old to the United States. They would have to emigrate under a quota based on the country of birth. I was twenty years old, but suddenly I decided to become under eighteen.

I had to figure out, though, what day was supposed to be my new birthday. If I made myself too young, they might allow an older youth to go first. If I made myself too old, I might not even get to go.

So we tried to find out how many had already signed up. I decided that the best thing would be for my birthday to be sometime in August, because the cut-off date for leaving was in September. My birthday became August 12, 1929, making me almost three years younger than I was.

I found out that because of the quotas I could not get in either as a Hungarian or a Romanian. So I applied as a German. I now was born in Germany, not Romania. This meant that I would need a birth certificate. So I decided to find a city where all the records had been destroyed, and nobody would be able to verify a birth one way or another. Consequently, I became documented as born in Breslau.

I refused to change my last name. But my first name was changed.

I had previously been registered with the American authorities under my real name, Nathan Tessler. But now, if anyone went to the American consulate and checked, they would learn that the Nathan

Tessler seeking to go to America was a lot younger than the one in the records. So for the committee I would have to have a different identity. I picked the name Robert, Robert Tessler. I wanted a first name beginning with a letter that was not too close to N.

I had to be interviewed by the committee so they could determine if I was who I said I was, and why I wanted to go to America. When you came to the office for the interview, you had to go up to a guard to be announced to the person in charge. I had been told through the grapevine exactly what to say, how to pretend that I was young, and to be clean shaven. I even wore clothes to make me look younger. When I got to the guard, he asked me what my name was, and I said Rudolph Tessler. I had forgotten my new first name was supposed to be Robert. So, in July of 1947 in Munich, I changed my papers to read Rudolph Tessler.

On August 12, I finally received the papers necessary to leave Germany. My brother Mendel was still in a hospital. My brother Buroch was a follower of the Klausenburger Rabbi. My father was running his restaurant. The day would come when we all would be reunited. But now was the time for me to leave.

I set out from the port of Bremerhaven on about September 13, 1947, on a ship named after a well-known American war correspondent, the *Ernie Pyle.*

On September 21, 1947, I arrived in America.

In America

I don't know why, but we didn't dock immediately. The ship stayed out in the New York harbor. On what we were to learn was Manhattan Island, we could see lots of yellow cars moving. What's going on? we wondered. Is everything there yellow? They were taxis, we were told.

We had arrived on a Saturday afternoon. As it grew darker, the excitement aboard the ship increased. There were close to five hundred of us, and most had been seasick during the crossing. That included me, but only for a few days, nothing serious. It was Sunday morning before we docked. All of us were supposed to be orphans. Some had relatives to greet them. Most had no one. Different organizations— the Hebrew Immigrant Aid Society (HIAS), the American JOINT Distribution Committee, and the American Children's Committee— took most of the passengers.

The group I was with was housed in a former convent at 661 Caldwell Avenue in the Bronx. And we were pampered. We had Corn Flakes and Rice Krispies! Out on the street, we could see vendors peddling three pounds of apples for a quarter. Along with the others, I was taken to a store where the people from the American Committee bought me a suit and a hat. Then I went to another store and got a pair of Thom McCann shoes. I remember it so well. We were all dressed up, with no place to go.

Life where we were staying was wonderful. In the morning we would have Corn Flakes and hard-boiled eggs, bread and coffee. We couldn't believe it, the variety and the quantity of food was wonderful.

There were foods we had never seen. I had never seen a banana, and none of us knew how to go about eating a grapefruit. Then the social workers got involved and talked to us about how to cope with our new environment and about our schooling and plans for the future. But we didn't need all that stuff. They talked theory, but we had the experience.

On that first Sunday evening a man by the name of Lebovitz showed up at the convent. He was originally from Viseu and now he was very active in the Marmaros Society of New York. My father was the president of the Marmaros Society in Munich. Lebovitz had heard that a ship was arriving with Jewish children from DP camps, and he was curious and anxious to help them. There were several of us from the same part of Marmaros who had come to the United States to live with relatives. When he learned I was there, he expressed concern that my uncles had not come to get me. "What's going on?" he asked, and then added, "They don't care. They're rich. They think they can do what they want. They don't participate in the Marmaros Society activities anyway."

He put five bucks in my pocket. It replaced the money my father had given me when I left Germany. On the ship a Western Union representative had asked if any of us wanted to send a telegram. So I sent one telling my father that I had arrived safely. That was the end of my first five dollars. As a result, I had no money when I arrived. Then I met Mr. Lebovitz. I was suddenly rich.

After that I was constantly buying apples and ice cream—Good Humor bars that were sold out on the street by the Good Humor men. Each bar cost a nickel.

As for my uncles, they did not know I was coming. They were never told.

Regardless, the next morning my Uncle Peter showed up with my cousin Harold. Mr. Lebovitz had called my uncle to tell him that his nephew had arrived. Harold was an assistant corporation counsel for New York City. A tall, husky guy, he was the son of my Uncle Isadore.

Uncle Peter started to cross-examine me. "Who is your father? Who was your grandmother?" He wanted to make sure I was not a phony. I passed muster. Uncle Peter said I was OK.

"Let's go," he said.

"What are you talking about?" I asked. "Where am I going?"

"Let's go," he repeated. "I don't have all day. Take your things and come."

Then my cousin Harold looked at him. "Pete," he said, "he isn't going. The kid is not going with you. Don't you see?"

"What do you mean he's not going?" my uncle asked. "I'm taking him with me."

I was adamant. I wasn't going, I told him. I refused because I was very independent. I had my own agenda, and to live with my uncle was not on it.

A few days later he came back to take me out to dinner.

I was at the convent for a couple of weeks. Later those of us who had no relatives (my records showed that I was an orphan) were sent to foster homes.

I did not know what a foster home was. I wound up in New Rochelle just outside New York City with a family named Cohen. The Cohens, who owned a haberdashery, had a history of helping people. In the 1930s they took in a Jewish refugee from Germany, kept him for several years, and put him through school. I was lucky to have wound up there.

But I didn't like it. I went to New Rochelle High School. I knew just a few words of English. I was a twenty-one-year-old senior in high school with a record showing that I was eighteen. And I was big, naturally, and tall for my age of eighteen.

But the English teacher helped me. She made each student buy a copy of the *New York Times* every day and read it. That's how I learned English. Still, I wasn't happy. I was there about six months but could not cope with all the restrictions of school. By then, because of what I had experienced, I was many generations removed from the high school students of New Rochelle. I learned quite a bit of English, but I didn't fit in. I went to visit my old DP friends as often as I could.

At that time, the intersection of Delancey and Essex Streets on the Lower East Side was the gathering place. On Sunday afternoons everybody was there, everybody who recently had come to America. It was a ritual. You would go there, meet, and then go to Rattner's, a big cafeteria-type restaurant, or to one of the many delicatessens. You would spend many hours there. It was a way of communicating, of keeping in touch. But, after a while, I decided that this also was not for me.

In Munich I had attended university classes on and off, trying to learn textile engineering. I never got to the point of knowing enough, but I knew that I wanted to be a textile engineer. In Philadelphia there was an excellent textile engineering school. My Uncle Peter said he would help me go there if I were willing to give up my religion. He said this because, among Jews like him in America, religion was viewed as old-fashioned. In America you were expected to be willing to work on the Sabbath and Jewish holidays. If you wanted to be religious, forget about it. You were wasting your time. When I said I did not want to go to the Philadelphia school under that condition, he was insulted. He was a self-made, very wealthy man; he demanded to know how I could say that. How I could refuse him, he could not understand. He was used to always getting his own way. But I was very independent and was not going to do anything other than what I wanted to do.

I still visited my uncle many times. I went to his home for dinners and he came to visit me. But it never was more than that. We became close, but not intimately close.

One day I decided to contact my cousin Harold. He lived in Jamaica on Long Island and had said that any time I wanted to live with his family, I was welcome. I called him and said, "Harold, I'm ready to come."

So I picked myself up and went to Harold's, planning to stay there until I found a job. Not long afterwards, maybe a few weeks, I found one in a knitting mill. In school in Munich, I learned a bit about how to run a weaving machine. I got the job, for a salary of thirty-eight dollars a week, moved out of Harold's, and took a room with a family that lived not far from him in Jamaica. It was March or April 1948.

My Uncle Isadore lived close by, and occasionally I went to his home for a meal. But I continued to be independent. I made thirty-eight dollars a week and it cost me about twenty-six dollars to live, leaving me with twelve dollars to save.

Later that year, just before the 1948 presidential election, the economy changed drastically. The textile industry was laying off people. A woman and I had been the last two hired, and we became the first two let go. Fortunately, I had a few dollars saved, so I could get by for a while. I took a job working in a luggage factory that made carrying cases for nuns' habits. After a while, however, I knew it was not the job for me. It was not what I wanted to do.

Then a friend of mine said, "There is a good way to make a few bucks. Why don't you become a waiter?" Lots of young people wanted to become waiters in the Catskills during the summer. Some of the DPs, who had arrived half a year ahead of me, had been waiters and wound up with about six hundred dollars saved for the season.

I didn't know anything about being a waiter. Still, I got a job at the Airmont Hotel in Suffern, New York. I took my first tray of dishes and, crash, I dropped it. But the owners gave me a break. Somehow, in the next few days I mastered it. At the end of the summer I came home with my pockets full of money. I went to a bank and opened an account. For me, that was a big thing. It was a beginning.

That year President Truman submitted a bill to Congress to allow one hundred thousand refugees to come to America outside the quota. Deducted from this number were refugees who had come and over-stayed their visas, and some who had come as preferential persons. The bill was passed and became effective in 1949. In March of that year, my father, who was fifty-one years old, and my brothers Buroch, age twenty-one, and Mendel, nineteen, came to America, to New York. I spent the winter of 1948-1949 as a waiter in a hotel in Florida. I came back to New York in April after the season was over. We were together again for the first time in eighteen months.

After the winter working in Florida, I had some money saved. With it I bought a produce store for my father in the Williamsburg section of Brooklyn. It was at 37 Lee Avenue. My father and brothers lived on the second floor and the store was downstairs.

I looked around for something else to do, because the store was not for me. I discovered a way to make money in South America by im-porting cars made in the United States. So I took a trip to Brazil and Uruguay. You could make a four-thousand-dollar profit on a two-thousand-dollar American car sold in Brazil. If you sold a Cadillac, you could make eight thousand dollars. I also made money selling gold chains. Almost everyone in Brazil wore a gold necklace with a cross on it. The factory that made the machines that manufactured the chains was in Offenbach, Germany. Because there was no peace treaty between Brazil and Germany, a German businessman could not do business in Brazil. I was able to arrange for the purchase of a machine that made the chains, and for a mechanic to travel from Germany to Rio de Janeiro to train people to operate it. Even though my papers identified me as a German, I found that Brazil was almost like Romania. It was just a question of price. For a price, Germans were permitted to enter and do business.

Back in America, I made the arrangements for the chain-making machine to be purchased in Germany and shipped to Rio. But at the end of June 1950, the Korean War began, and I was of draft age. That was the end of the gold chain business. I was not able to be away from the United States for more than thirty days or I would lose any right to return as a permanent resident alien.

In the fall of 1950 I was approaching my twenty-fourth birthday. I was called before a draft board and, because of my poor eyesight, classified as 4-F, but it was made clear to me that my "disability" would not preclude me from being called at a future date if needed. They kept reclassifying people depending on how badly they wanted them. I found out, however, that farmers were exempt from going. So I bought a farm near Frenchtown, New Jersey. I had seen enough of war. My father and my brother Mendel also became farmers. I was there now and then, but I didn't care for it very much.

In the meantime, I met and married the woman who would be the center and the compass of my life.

In the fall of 1950, after my return from South America, Edith was introduced to me by a cousin of mine who had been with her in Sweden after the war. Edith came to this country on February 11, 1948, almost five months after I did. She was the youngest survivor of a family of ten children. Her parents and seven brothers and sisters were murdered at Auschwitz, Bergen-Belsen, and Muhldorf, as were her brother-in-law, nieces, and nephews. Edith was one of twenty-five thousand Jewish women who were prisoners at Bergen-Belsen at the war's end. She was seventeen when the camp was liberated. Many of the survivors were taken on Red Cross ships to Sweden, where they were invited to recuperate as guests of the government. Edith was so weak that she had to be carried on a stretcher. Her stay in Sweden lasted almost three years. Her sister, Rose, lived with her in New York. At that time, a brother, Sandor, was still in Hungary.

After a courtship of a few months, we were married on July 4, 1951. The ceremony was in Chateau Garden, a beautiful place on Houston Street in the Lower East Side. It was an outdoor wedding, and it cost me $585 for everything, including the music, flowers, and drinks. The wedding might be described as modest in comparison to the more elaborate ones of today. About a hundred people attended. We had very few relatives still alive and who lived in America.

My wife had been living with Rose and her husband, Marvin Davies, on the Lower East Side. When we met, it was love at first sight. She was a very delicate, gentle lady and still is. She was very hesitant, though, about meeting me, because I came from an area where the people were a little bit less cultured than those in her native region.

Edith had come from Papa, a town in Hungary that is a two-and-a-half-hour drive west of Budapest. Her family, which had lived there for almost two hundred years, was very wealthy and very prominent, among the elite of the Jewish community, not only in their town, but throughout the whole area. Her great-grandfather was the Chasam Sofer, the renowned chief rabbi of Bratislava, one of the world's greatest rabbis. In his time he was one of the greatest men alive. At a very young age, eight or nine, he was recognized as an important scholar. He became a very learned man. He was accepted by all segments of Judaism, whether they were German, Polish, Romanian, or Ukrainian Jews. He was accepted even though he was an Ashkenazi, having been born in Frankfurt.

Edith was from a distinguished family, and I was a plain ordinary guy from a primitive area. In the normal course of events we would have never married, given the difference in our backgrounds, my wife's Hungarian Jewish aristocracy and my somewhat primitive Marmaros Jewish existence. She had no mother or father to advise her, so she was hesitant about marrying. When she met my father, she took to him easily. He loved her very much. She would become closer to him than a daughter.

After our wedding, I took her to the farm in New Jersey, but she never liked it. She had never lived on a farm. In fact, I don't think she had ever been on one. As the youngest daughter in her family, she had been pampered; they had servants and a very comfortable life.

My father worked on the farm in his boots, milking the cows and caring for the chickens. Buroch was not there; he had married. Mendel, however, was. Like my father, Mendel wore boots and overalls. He would often come in the house as dirty as any hard-working farmer. Edith had a rough time getting used to such a different world.

The farmhouse was large, and a beautiful garden surrounded it. But the interior of the house had been painted rather hastily by Mendel and me on the day before my wedding. We had left a few splotches—the job was not done by an interior decorator. Edith found it all very uncomfortable.

We stayed on the farm for less than a year. Then we took an apartment in the Crown Heights section of Brooklyn, which at the time was considered to be very nice. We were there for less than a year. On May 25, 1952, our daughter Florence was born in Brooklyn.

For Passover in 1953, when Florence was eleven months old, the three of us went to Chicago to visit Edith's sister and her husband, who now lived there. We stayed. We had nothing to lose. Marvin helped me find a job at Hart, Schaffner and Marx. The pay was eighty-five dollars a week, which was good. We found a giant apartment in Albany Park on Chicago's northwest side. It was above a store and beautifully furnished with many antiques. The old lady who owned it spoke only Yiddish, so my daughter began learning Yiddish.

Meanwhile, many other Jews were moving into the neighborhood. One of the stores beneath us was a barber shop, and the barber was Gordon Klasky, who had been at Auschwitz until he was evacuated late in 1944. He told me how, in order to stay alive, he shaved the Germans at the camp and cut their hair. He has been my barber ever since, and for my sons and grandsons as well.

Our son, David, was born on April 9, 1956. By then we had our own small place with four rooms. I became a cloth cutter and learned textile designing for men's clothing as well. I became a designer. But I was always itching. The job was not good enough. No matter what I earned in those days, it was not enough to provide what we needed and what we wanted. So I went into my own business on the side, selling bolt ends of cloth, and many times made several hundred dollars a week extra doing that.

Friends I made in those days are still friends. One of them was a tailor at Hart, Schaffner and Marx, Tom Luchetta. He still makes suits for me, and our friendship continues.

I decided to look around for other business ventures. I went into the vending machine business with Erwin "Red" Weiner. We did so well that I had to give up my full-time job at Hart, Schaffner & Marx.

I gradually started to go into real estate. The large vending machine companies grew even bigger and the smaller ones either merged or sold out. The small ones could not continue because of the competition. We needed a lot of capital. I had no way of coming up with more, so I decided to sell the business. I sold it and went to work for Mutual of New York as an insurance agent. Gradually I worked my way up to operating a multi-line insurance business until, in the 1960s, I had an agency of my own. Nevertheless, the business did not offer opportunity, because you only made money by selling insurance. You received the commissions, but you had no way of making money through investments. The more you worked, the more money you made, but it did not provide the opportunity to make major money.

At that point the nursing home business started to develop into an industry. I began to invest, and then I acquired a small piece of ownership in a nursing home. My involvement was passive until we bought the first nursing home that I managed. Then I began easing out of the insurance business and eventually left it completely.

Soon I became totally involved in nursing homes. Simultaneously, however, I continued developing real estate. I bought an old industrial building, rehabbed it, and sold it. I built condo buildings. I bought land. But mostly I rehabbed multistory commercial buildings. In Chicago old buildings could be purchased for very little money. We then restored the buildings to their original exteriors, upgraded their interiors, and sold them. We developed the Mergenthaler Building in Printers Row in the South Loop, and Institute Place on the Near

North Side. In the vicinity of the Merchandise Mart we acquired old loft buildings, and buildings on Wabash Avenue, Lake Street, and the Near West Side. These were large properties.

The biggest was the former Milwaukee Railroad building at Fullerton and Southport Avenues on the North Side. It was a one-hundred-year-old building five hundred feet long. When we acquired it, its interior looked like a ruin of the war. But it was a landmark. We restored it, and we made it a continuum care health center, the first of its kind in the country. It's now a nursing home with retirement apartments, a home health agency, and a geriatric clinic.

In Israel, in the town of Netanya, is a settlement called Kiryat Sanz. The settlement was built by the Klausenburg Rabbi. It includes schools from elementary to post-graduate, as well as housing, a hotel—a whole complex, mostly for religious Jews from Israel and America. It also includes a hospital and the Tessler School of Nursing. The U.S. government gave half of the money, and I gave the other half. We are very proud of the nursing school. Its students graduate with the highest achievement records of any nursing school in Israel.

As demanding as business was on my time and energy, my family took precedence in everything. In Chicago, my family and the family of my wife's sister, Rose, were very, very close. Rose and Marvin have four lively sons. Our kids and their kids grew up together. The kids really had two mothers. Their kids ate with ours and ours with them. They slept over at each family's home. It was like one family. It was a warm reminder of our lost world in Romania and Hungary.

My brother Buroch stayed in New York. He was the first of the brothers to marry. He and his wife had a daughter and five sons. He has many grandchildren.

For many years Buroch has been known in the New York area as "Mr. Doctor." Anyone in need of a medical specialist, domestic or foreign, has been able to contact him, and a specialist has been provided. Whether the person has or does not have money, he or she is taken care of. If people have money, they pay. If they don't, Buroch sees to it that the money is made available. He has contacts with internationally renowned medical people at Mount Sinai, Beth Israel, and other hospitals in New York and elsewhere. I do not know how all this came about except that in our family it is a family tradition to help anyone in need. This aspect of Buroch goes back many years and is something that he has worked at day and night.

Buroch and a partner, a friend and former schoolmate of mine, own several large buildings. From his time in Munich with the Klausenburg Rabbi, Buroch also continues to be deeply involved in the Klausenburger movement and actually builds institutions for it, multimillion-dollar operations that he supervises. When the Rabbi passed away, Buroch became executor of his estate.

I see my brother often. We are quite close. His children and mine are together at all family affairs. His children are all scholars and business people. They continue the tradition of Hebrew names in their own families. Buroch's first wife died more than fifteen years ago, and he is remarried.

My brother Mendel also lives in New York City. Before coming here, Mendel had been in several hospitals in Germany as a result of the gunshot wound that splintered one of his thigh bones. In the United States, his condition improved thanks to good medical care, but to this day he still suffers from the wound. Part of the bullet is still in him. He was with my father on the farm which we had in New Jersey, and he loved that work. When the farm was sold in 1954, he became an offset printer and for many years operated his own successful business.

Mendel and his wife have a daughter and two sons.

When my father came with my brothers to New York, I bought the farm in New Jersey for two reasons. The first was the draft. The second was so my father could be occupied. When the farm was sold, he moved at age fifty-six to New York and went to work as a shamas (sexton) in a synagogue. He continued at that work well into his eighties. All of those years he was healthy. He also took a job working in a men's clothing store and was active at it until he was eighty-seven.

Every morning he had a shot of whiskey. In about 1952, he remarried. His wife was about three years older but looked much younger. She came from Poland and had three children by her previous husband, who had been lost in Russia.

We went to visit him many times, and he came to Chicago for several family affairs. He and his wife spent the winters in Florida. When he reached the age of ninety, he could no longer make the Florida trip. As his health declined, he began to need more attention, and I wanted to bring him to Chicago. But the family felt he should remain in New York, because that is where most of his family was. So he was placed in a nursing home in Brooklyn.

We had a man with him around the clock, and not a single meal passed without one of my nephews or my brothers there. One would be with him in the morning, one at lunch, and one at dinner, for seven days a week.

I was in New York frequently, as was my wife. She was very close to my father. My wife needed a family very much. He was like her father as well as mine. He was everything.

When he was ninety-two, his mind began trailing off at times. One of my nephews had a great talent for cheering him up—he was the morning guy. My father would talk about the old days and my nephew would prod him, "Tell me more, tell me more about the olden days." Many times he cheered him by recalling that my father had been a disciple of a great rabbi in Romania, the Viznitz Rabbi's grandfather. My father opened up when he talked about him. "Oh my rabbi," he would say. "My rabbi." That was medicine that cheered him.

Still, he gradually declined, and then passed away on November 4, 1991. It was about three weeks before his ninety-third birthday. My son Mordie was with him at the end. I was there on a Sunday, and he died two days later. I had told my sons I would be with him on Sunday, then David on Monday, and Mordy on Tuesday. My father closed his eyes and passed away. He was buried in Israel in Bne Braq in a family plot in the Viznitz cemetery, which he had bought many years earlier.

His wife passed away four days before him on the previous Friday. She was buried in Jerusalem in a plot she bought. It was not known to us that she had made those arrangements. Edith and I saw her in the hospital a few days before she died.

The Jewish people have a custom of naming a child after a close departed relative, usually one of the child's great-grandparents. But after the Holocaust the survivors had no parents, so they named their children after their murdered parents. I always wanted our kids to have Hebrew names, like my sons David and Mordecai. My daughter Florence is named after my wife's mother. David is named after my wife's father. His children have the names of my wife's mother and father, and my mother and father. The only family that has the names of all the grandparents is David's. For us, it is very important that parents continue the names of close, deceased family members.

My grandchildren have living grandparents, so, in keeping with tradition, if they want to name a child, they would have to use those of my deceased parents or grandparents. But the current generation was frequently named after a grandparent who was not alive.

Hasidism has always played a role in my life. We were inculcated in it at home. When I came to America, I could have done what many other people did. I had nobody. I had no discipline to follow. There was nobody to tell me what to do or what not to do. My father came here but, by then, he was a broken person. He did not speak the language. He had a hard time coping. I was twenty years old with no real guidance, lacking a sense of responsibility and a sense of determining right from wrong. My uncle told me that if I wanted to become a textile engineer, I would have to forget about being observant. I would have to forget about being Orthodox. I could never have done that. My Hasidic and family upbringing was too strong.

I needed to marry a woman who was religious and came from a strong family background. My wife did not come from a Hasidic background. But she was religious, and she came from a strong family. My wife's family emphasized the values of family and communal responsibility. I never knew my father-in-law, but I know that every Saturday morning he went to pray at seven o'clock. At nine he returned home and ate breakfast. After that he went to visit the Jewish hospital in town every Saturday. That was his custom. He did not have to do it. He did it because he wanted to set an example for his children. My wife, even as a six-year-old, tagged along and saw what he did.

When we moved to Chicago and as our family began to grow, my wife and I decided our family had to have a religious base. Fortunately, my wife was a major influence. Sometimes a man marries a woman who contradicts her husband, and they do not see eye to eye on many things. Among them are how to bring up a family and their religious outlook. We have never had those problems.

It has been said that in the Holocaust G-d abandoned the Jews. It has been asked how a Jew who experienced those years could ever be as devoted as he or she might have been previously.

Elie Wiesel wrote that, after fifty years, he was making peace with G-d, that he was, in effect, forgiving G-d. I remember that in one of his books he had a dialogue with G-d and said that G-d was not in the camps. How could there be a G-d, he asked, if all those things were allowed to happen? Not a day went by without one of the guards taunting: "Where is your G-d?" When a guard beat you, he said, "Now let your G-d help you."

Wiesel had many quarrels with G-d, to the point that he did not accept Him. Even though his father was a pious Hasidic Jew, Wiesel was not at all religious after the war. He was secular. He went to the Sorbonne and then met some people I know who had a great influence on him. Gradually he began saying, well, as smart as I am and as much as I know, maybe I don't know everything. Questioning himself, he asked, "Would I take back anything that I have written thirty or forty years ago?" His answer was "No. That is what I wrote and what I felt at a particular time. What I feel now is different."

I did not have doubts, but questions. Without believing in G-d, without believing and having faith, you could not survive. Nobody could have survived. No matter what they tell you, they did not survive without faith. A man died in my arms when he said, "It's no use. I'm not going to make it." When you lost faith and hope, it was all over. How can you possibly explain it any other way? How can you

survive the atrocities and come to America as a twenty-year-old and
be normal, not crippled psychologically or emotionally, and continue
on? Yet an estimated 80 percent of the seventy-two thousand concentration camp survivors who came to the United States have been very
successful people.

I had my questions, but the faith that I had as a youngster held. It
kept nurturing in my spirit what needed to be nurtured. Had I married a different woman, my path would have been different, I'm sure,
because the greatest influence on a man is his wife.

But, yes, there were questions. I still have questions. I have no an-
swers. At the same time, I say that the answer to what happened is
how else, without the existence of G-d, could a human being go
through what he went through and remain a normal, thriving human
being with a family?

There were many people who became shell-shocked and self-cen-
tered and said, "To hell with everything. Look at how cruel the world
is. There is no way that I am going to do anything for anybody." If you
don't act that way, then obviously there is a G-d. Otherwise, how else
can you account for it? How else can you explain? A human being is
so resilient that you bounce back, and it happens quickly. A year or
two or three is quick.

Have I come across many survivors who were permanently dis-
abled emotionally? No. But they overlooked their children. The over-
whelming majority of the children of the survivors are not religious. I
don't know the reason. It could have been that their anchor, their family and their upbringing, was not strong enough. Most of the survivors
of the Holocaust no longer believe in G-d. At the same time, I believe
they have their doubts about whether they are right. Somewhere
along the line, as a result of their loss of belief, their children have had
problems because they did not receive the proper upbringing. Their
children did not receive the anchor of faith.

I know families of survivors whose children have had psychological
problems because of self-doubt about their lives. You go to work and
you make money and you spend it. You give it to the kids and you
send them to school, but that is not enough. The kids can have the best

education, but if you don't give them morals and ethics, it's worthless. It is worse to be an educated person without morals than to be uneducated and have morals.

It has been more than fifty years since the liberation and the end of the war. The survivors are now all old people. Many come to gatherings marking those long-ago events because they feel that something they have done might not be right. They are seeking something that will give them satisfaction. Something is missing in their lives. It is gnawing at them. Something is not right with their children.

My wife and I have always been members of a synagogue as a way of life. We do not keep to the external manifestations of the Hasidic tradition, the physical appearance and clothing, in my family. But our faith and identity stay clear and strong. We feel part of America, but retain all of the essential, core beliefs of our ancestors.

Hasidim are rigorously faithful to their traditions, but at the same time they are flexible and accommodating. The historic success of the Hasidic movement derived from the fact that it was flexible and non-dogmatic. Everybody was accepted, regardless of appearance.

The heart and spirit of the Hasidic movement survived the Holocaust. Hasidic Jews who left Europe after the war were still religiously inclined because of their upbringings and backgrounds. They were searching to re-create their destroyed communities. But when the war was over, most of the great Hasidic leaders were dead. The rabbis who survived, by and large, were broken people. The Hasidic movement after the war did not have sufficient strength, nor did it have giants to guide it, men like the Chasam Sofer, my wife's great-great-grandfather. "I am not worried about Jewish law," he said. "I know it, and the law is with me." He had confidence.

After the war you did not have leaders with that kind of confidence—except for a few rare people like the Klausenburg Rabbi, a great authority. He was a magnetic individual, and he knew the law. As a result, he attracted many disciples, but they were very much on the political right, very dogmatic.

There was a great rabbi in New York called the Satmar rabbi. He was a prominent scholar, but he was very much on the right and an outspoken anti-Zionist. He said Zionism was a movement that was alien to Judaism. As a result of views like his, the traditions and way of life of Hasidic Jews in Europe were not re-created here for almost two generations. Today there are a number of Hasidic Jews in America, but they are very much on the right, and very much isolated in their own communities and in their own way of life.

I would describe myself and my sons as modern, not Hasidic. But I still like the Hasidic way of life and I have supported it. We don't wear the clothing and don't maintain the requisite appearance. But the spirit is there.

I have been asked if I adhere to the same spirit as I did when I was a boy. I do. I love my faith and tradition and think that the warmth of Judaism comes from the Hasidic way of life. That spirit is being carried to Ashkenazic Jews because of its warmth.

Return to Viseu

I have made four trips from America back to Viseu, the most recent in the summer of 1995. The first was in 1972, twenty-five years after I left Germany on the *Ernie Pyle*. I could not go when the children were small; they took precedence over everything. My work, my business, and my wife's activities revolved around our family. We took the children into consideration in everything we did or didn't do.

But as you become more settled, you start to think about your past. So despite the risks involved in going to a Communist-controlled country, we embarked for Bucharest.

Romania was as corrupt as ever. The chief rabbi in Romania after the war, Rabbi Rosen, was also a member of the Romanian senate and had great prestige. As a result, he was able to help most of the Jews of Romania to leave for Israel. But for every migrating Jew, there was a cash payment to Romanian officials. I am sure some of the money came from the various international Jewish organizations.

For those Jews who remained in Romania, the rabbi saw to it that their needs were met. In a number of cities he established old-age homes that included kosher kitchens providing kosher food in a Jewish communal setting. The money came from the American JOINT Distribution Committee. In 1972, the synagogue in Bucharest was open. But the oppression was obvious. Almost every corner had an armed soldier.

Jews who travel have a habit of contacting other Jews in places they visit. One of the reasons is to find out what is going on, where the synagogue and kosher restaurants are. The second reason is that you may need help. You usually find out what is happening in a country if you are in touch with the right people. One of the addresses I had in Romania was that of a famous criminal lawyer who lived in Bucharest. We called him and said we wanted to visit. We had been asked to extend regards to him from lawyers in the United States.

"Hold on," the lawyer said. "I can't talk to you over the phone, but we can meet. Where are you staying?"

"The Inter-Continental," I said.

"I will meet you across the street from it," the lawyer said. Then he described how he looked and asked how he could identify me. It was like in a movie. "You walk by three times and then I will walk by three times and then we will say hello to each other," he told me.

Across from the hotel there was an airline office. A man walked by and then my wife and I did the same. We asked if he was the lawyer and he said yes, immediately adding, "Let's go." He did not want to talk to us there. "Come," he said, motioning, and he took us to his apartment. We went in, and he pulled the phone line from the jack and turned on the water faucets. "Everything is bugged," he warned us. "Everything."

You could feel the oppression. Here was a successful criminal lawyer who was able to earn what was a high income for anyone at that time who was not a government official. But because so much of the average person's income went to the government in taxes, clients often paid an attorney in kind, with a chicken, a calf, a lamb. They traded for his services, and the lawyer, in turn, made trades to the butcher to get meat. That's how business was conducted.

From Bucharest, Edith and I had plane tickets to Baia Mare, the town with the airport closest to Viseu. We arrived at the Bucharest airport well ahead of the scheduled departure time, but we were told the plane was gone. This was hardly a busy airport. We could see a toothless porter in a uniform smiling at us. He was sizing us up, and I could tell he was thinking that, because of us, he was going to make some real money that day. We were a couple of foreigners, a couple of Americans. He could see we had nice suitcases. And he knew that our plane had not left.

The porter ran out of the terminal to a small, eighteen-passenger plane parked nearby, ran up the steps to the plane's open door, grabbed a manifest from within, and came running back toward the terminal, smiling, with the manifest in his hands. Then he knocked at the agent's window and waved at us. All the while the ticket agent kept telling us that it was too late. "No, no," shouted the grinning porter. "Open up. It's not closed. I have the manifest and the plane will not go unless these guys go. Either let these people go on it," he warned, "or nobody will go." The girl at the ticket counter had no choice.

It was the way of life. Everybody wanted to make a few extra bucks. As I walked from the terminal to the waiting plane, I gave the guy a dollar and a pack of cigarettes, and that probably equaled a good part of his income for at least a month. We then took off for Baia Mare. On the plane you did not sit in seats alongside one another facing forward. You sat on benches lining the sides of the plane.

Baia Mare is a mining town that had become a big city of approximately one hundred thousand, with the usual dark, drab, gray-looking cement-block apartment buildings. They all looked alike, the way the projects did all over Eastern Europe. As the plane hovered over the city, I asked what had happened to the open land that was once there. Suddenly, I could see a patch down below. It was the airport.

Before we left Baia Mare to go to Viseu, we had another unusual experience. The town had a tourist office headed by a German who had lived in Viseu. At about midnight, this German knocked on the door of our hotel room. "Can I come in?" he asked. My wife told him he couldn't. "What do you want?" she asked. He proceeded to inquire whether we had any clothing for sale—jeans, pants, underwear, anything. My wife said we didn't but that she would talk to him in the morning.

The next day she told him that she had left a straw hat at the hotel in Bucharest and that, if he was willing to go there, he could have it. She gave him a piece of paper telling the people back at the hotel that this man could have the hat. He actually traveled there to get it. That is how poor those people were.

Baia Mare is one hundred kilometers west of Viseu. Between the two towns is what must be some of the most beautiful scenery in the world. The route is a circuitous one, with a winding road that twists its way through heavily forested mountains. It is still great logging country. It's all pine and spruce and beautiful, but also very primitive. It is how G-d created it.

When our driver pulled into Viseu, everything seemed different to me. I did not recognize anything. Everything seemed so small. At the beginning of 1944, Viseu had been a real town, the most important community in our area. To enter it, you had to cross a bridge over the Viseu River. At the river's edge there was a train station. Now the station looked like a little nothing. The bridge looked tiny. Even the river seemed diminished.

We drove to the center of town. I didn't recognize anything—nothing whatsoever. The last time I had been back, in September of 1945, there were still the burned remnants of the buildings that had been there before the retreating Germans torched the town's business center. Now I recognized nothing until we came to the main synagogue. That was still standing.

My uncle's store had never been rebuilt. Nothing was recognizable. We drove around the town several times. I began to see a few things out of the past, but none were as I remembered. Even the lions in front of the synagogue, the ones that were our local landmarks, had become small like everything else. We learned that there was a man by the name of Mendel Friedman who had lived in Viseu all those years and was still there. We were told that it would not be difficult to find him, that we should just ask around. I wanted to go to the cemetery, and he could be helpful in getting there.

We drove up to his house and found him praying. The front door of the house was open and a farmer was standing there. It was June but still cool. The farmer was standing while Friedman was praying, and his wife was making breakfast. The stove she was using was probably the same one that had been in the house for the past two hundred years. It was a built-in hearth in which wood was burned. On top of it were several ring-openings through which the heat came. You used three rings for a large pot, two for a smaller pot, and one for the smallest. The woman was making mamaliga, cereal made from cornmeal, the national food. To make it, you put water in a pot and bring it to a boil. Then you put in flour and stir.

The woman, who was wearing a long black dress with a kerchief on her head, invited us to have breakfast. So we sat down and had some of the cereal and cheese. It was the healthiest food you can get, completely natural. When he finished his prayers, Friedman reminded me where the cemetery was and then accompanied us there.

At the edge of the town rise the foothills of the Carpathian Mountains. The cemetery was on the side of one of them. It has been there for many, many years. Long ago people from the nearby villages, as well as the town's people, were buried there to make sure that their monuments would be safe from desecration.

There was a small Romanian military camp nearby, with a few barracks. Soldiers in the camp could see us drive up to the cemetery gate in the chauffeur-driven Mercedes we had hired, and they were quite suspicious. Not many cars came down that road. We were watched very carefully.

The cemetery ground had been quite saturated by rain, and we sank down a few inches as we walked. I found the graves of my grandfather and one of his brothers. The tombstones were in disarray. Lettering had fallen off. I later got a man to fix it. I could not, however, find my grandmother's grave. She died seven years before my grandfather; I did not know exactly where she was buried.

After going to the cemetery, I went to see my house. A room had been added to it, but the facade was the same. Across a courtyard from the house was where our store had been. The building still stood, but now there was no store.

Just as we were knocking on the door, a woman ran toward us from across the street, calling out, "Tuli. Hey Tuli." Tuli was my nickname. It was an older woman. "You're Tuli," she said. "Aren't you?" Before I could answer, she asked, "How is Esther?"

The woman was the grandmother of the SS guard who had greeted my mother when we arrived at Auschwitz. I almost broke down because my mother was such a loved woman. I remember she used to make a special honey cake for that German family every Christmas. The old woman remembered us. She now lived across the street from our house.

She apparently had no idea of what had transpired. She knew that our family no longer existed in Viseu. She knew that something had happened, but she had not been told about the concentration camps. I am sure she was aware that Jews had been killed, but not those in the family she once knew.

There was a woman living in our house. She invited us in, and Edith and I went in and sat down. The house was basically the same as it had been, but it looked much smaller. Almost three decades had gone by. It seemed like a thousand years. Everything outside the house had been transformed.

We spent little time in my former home. There was no great feeling one way or the other. I never went to see the other house, the house across the courtyard where my grandparents lived. We walked around the muddy garden and then we left.

We then went with Friedman to see the synagogue. It was locked. Hardly anyone ever went there.

The main synagogue had been built with an ark, the repository for scrolls of the Torah, that was the most famous one in that part of the world. The ark was still there, but it had been greatly neglected. There were so many leaks in the synagogue roof that it seemed to be raining inside.

The synagogue had arches and columns done in the style of the Italian Renaissance. The structure itself was not large, holding only a few hundred people. But the ceilings and walls had expansive and beautiful paintings depicting events and people in Jewish history. Now all that was neglected. Part of the walls had been painted over in dull gray. The pulpit was in bad shape. There was a small sanctuary that was used from time to time, but there was almost never a minyan. Only about eight Jews lived in town, and not all of them were religious—only about eight Jews where, in 1944, there had been almost five thousand.

With Friedman's help, from that synagogue I obtained three brass candlesticks, which I took with me and still have. From its sanctuary, I have the cover of the ark.

Across from that synagogue was a smaller one, the one where those thousands of books had been put, from the floor to the ceiling, after the Germans had taken us away. Every Jewish house had many, many books. They had all been in the second synagogue when I came back in 1945. Now, in 1972, they were gone. Nothing was there. The building was now used as some kind of repair shop. I do not have the slightest idea what happened to all those books.

Some people might think it ironic that the Germans would burn down the center of the town and leave the main synagogue standing. It is my opinion that the Germans, who were running from the advancing Russians, ran out of time. As a result, they threw their fire bombs indiscriminately. They fled west on the main street, shooting, killing, and destroying. The Soviet army never occupied the town. They just went through. There was no actual battle in the town.

The large dormitory in Viseu, part of the former yeshiva, had been destroyed by the retreating Germans. In its place, when I came back on this visit, was a small apartment building. There also had once been a courtyard surrounded by the communal offices. It was where the rabbi, Mendel Hager, the judges, the slaughterer, and the shamas or sexton all lived. All of the weddings took place in that courtyard. Now that was gone. Everything had been destroyed.

Almost all of the Germans, who once made up one-third of Viseu's population, had either been chased away or had left voluntarily in 1945. Many had been put on trains headed for Siberia. Others went deep into Transylvania to cities such as Medias and Timisora where there were textile plants. But the Romanians did not welcome them. So some returned to Viseu.

Unlike in Czechoslovakia, very few Germans were ejected from Romania. The exceptions were those who had something to do with the atrocities and those whose sons volunteered for the SS. They were the ones shipped to Siberia. A substantial number of Germans, however, stayed in Romania. I don't know whether the ones who then occupied our house had gone away and come back, or whether they had stayed in Viseu all along.

We walked around the town a little bit, and my wife bought a handmade woolen sweater—you could still buy some. But that was it. We did not spend much time there.

We went back to Baia Mare by a different route, one that was even more rugged and scenic than the first and took much longer. From

Baia Mare we took a plane back to Bucharest. Our destination was Constanta, a famous resort city on the Black Sea and the main harbor for Romania as well as much of that part of the world.

We traveled to Constanta by train. The stations in the large cities of Europe are very big, and the trains are very long, with sections that are first class and second class, sometimes even third class. We had first-class tickets and several heavy suitcases. From Romania we were going to travel on to Israel.

The porter took us to what he said was the first-class section and deposited our luggage. But it was not our car, and it was second class. Our reserved seats were in the front of the train, but these seats were in the rear, and it was hot as hell. There was no air-conditioning. It must have been a hundred degrees. People filled the seats and were outside the compartment in the corridor. Every inch was jam-packed. You could not move. Meanwhile, somewhere on that train, our reserved, first class accommodations were empty.

Into the compartment came a man with a ticket that he said was for the seat I was in. But I decided I would pretend not to understand him. Nobody except Edith and I spoke English. So we just sat there while the man screamed that I had his seat. I told my wife that, whatever she did, she should not get up from her seat. The man kept screaming, but we continued to sit.

After a while I told my wife that I did not think it was fair, so I let the others put their suitcases up on the rack. Then, gradually, I admitted that things weren't right and that I was going to find another seat. I did not admit to the others that I did not really have a seat there, but I said that at least the man could sit for a while. Then I started to walk in search of first class. I not only had to climb over people and packages but livestock as well. Finally I reached the air-conditioned dining car midway in the train. By then I had decided I would not try to get to the first-class section, because it still was way at the other end of the train. It would have taken me half a day.

My wife never left her second-class seat, and I never got my seat back. It was an exhausting train trip.

When we eventually arrived at the hotel in Constanta, Edith hated it. It was terrible, definitely not the fine resort hotel that it was supposed to be. Ninety-nine percent of the occupants were Germans, and they all spoke German, which my wife did not like. This was a Communist country behind the Iron Curtain, but Germans, mostly from West Germany, traveled all over Europe even then. They had the money. For them a vacation in Romania was very cheap.

The next morning I went to the office of Tarom, the Romanian national airline, and asked if a plane was leaving for Bucharest. When I was informed there were no flights available, the usual sort of "gift" made two seats suddenly become open.

In dealing with anyone in the country, I never spoke Romanian, always German or English. I did not want them to know that I was a Romanian because, when I left, I was of draft age and I wasn't taking any chances—although I was now forty-five. The Communists had actually taken some people like me into the army. I never admitted I spoke Romanian.

When we finally reached Bucharest after a two-hour delay in departure, we wanted to leave for Israel on the first plane out. So we departed the following morning on a plane full of a group of Romanian Jews emigrating to Israel. Among them was a couple in their seventies with whom we attempted to make conversation. Not until the plane passed the halfway mark from Romania to Israel did they open up. They noticed my wife's wedding ring and were quite surprised. The woman had left hers behind, she said, because the government would not allow emigrants to take anything of value. She said she would have given her ring to us to carry if she had known we were foreigners.

The man told us that their son was chairman of the Romanian atomic energy commission. He informed us that anti-Semitism was beginning to emerge in the country. Quite a few of the old-time Communists had been Jews, but now the party was encouraging them to retire. He insisted, however, that their son was not afraid of anything and would retain his position. But they were not so sure about the Romanian government's intentions. Not until we had landed in Tel Aviv did the man give me a card telling me who he was. He was afraid right until the last minute.

My next three trips to Viseu were to show our children and grandchildren where their family had come from. And it always bothered me that I had been unable to find my grandmother's grave. This was the woman who used to give me two pieces of candy for knowing my lessons and who said that, because of it, I would remember and pray for her after she was gone. I had asked my father to describe where the grave was. Still, I failed to locate it.

In 1974, I again visited the synagogue in Viseu. It had continued to deteriorate and was in need of a lot of repairs. Another visitor, a man originally from Viseu who was then living in Belgium, and I enquired about the synagogue. We were told that it would cost twenty thousand dollars to fix the building, and that repairs must be done or the synagogue would have to be torn down. So we contacted the Viznitz Rabbi in Switzerland, for whom I had much respect, and asked what we should do.

"What is the synagogue needed for?" he asked. "Everyone in Viseu is very old. Today there may be eight Jews, next year six, and soon two. What then?" The Rabbi advised us to spend the money on something more constructive. But we all agreed that the ark should be saved. So the synagogue was torn down and the ark was stored in boxes in Bucharest. Also saved was a wooden candelabra that held 365 candles which had been converted from candlelight to electric lights, and the two landmark lions. Those objects, like the ark, were transported to Bucharest. Efforts I made to take them to Israel were unsuccessful. At one time I had the permission of both our State Department and the Romanian government to bring them to the United States. But the chief rabbi in Bucharest said no.

Edith and Mordy were with me. The trip was his bar mitzvah present. On our way home from Viseu, we drove to the Romanian city of Oradea on the Hungarian border. The driver who brought us there suggested we check into a hotel and proceed in the morning. That wasn't the deal, I said. We were supposed to meet a new driver, and he was going to take us on to Budapest with no delays. We would not be resting, I said, because I had to be in Budapest that night in order to do something the next morning. We had a schedule to meet.

The driver said the man scheduled to take us to Budapest did not want to go, but that he, the original driver, would, as he put it, "do something for us." That something was to bring us to the border only a few minutes away and arrange for a taxi to take us the 150 kilometers to Budapest. I said that if he would make the call and arrange for the taxi, everything would be all right. I claimed that I spoke neither Hungarian nor Romanian. He agreed to call and make the arrangements.

When we got to the border, there was no telephone that he could use. The nearest town in Hungary was fifteen kilometers away.

There were two border police, a captain and a lieutenant. The captain came to my wife, Mordy, and me and looked us over. Like most Romanians, he was jovial. He started to talk to us. I understood him but pretended that I didn't. Where did I want go? he asked. Bucharest? Budapest?

Then the lieutenant came over and decided to practice his few words of English on me. In English I told him to ask the captain if he had a car to take us to Budapest. When he did that, the captain said to us, "No problem. The lieutenant will drive the three of you to Budapest tonight."

The captain said he wanted a carton of cigarettes. My wife told him I didn't smoke. Then he said, "How about a Parker pen?" I told him I thought I could arrange that. I had one that cost about three dollars, and I gave it to him.

Just as the lieutenant was about to drive his car with us in it to Budapest, a bus with tourists from Yugoslavia pulled in. The lieutenant ran up to the bus and saw that it had three empty seats. The captain thereupon told the driver to take us to Budapest free of charge. Sure enough, we said good-bye to the captain and the lieutenant and got on the bus.

When we arrived in Budapest, the driver did not know his way. It was about midnight, and we were at the last stop of a trolley line. I got out of the bus and went to talk to a trolley motorman. "Listen," I said, "we have to go to the Inter-Continental Hotel." He said, "Follow me." I asked the driver where he had to go, and he said across the bridge. So we followed the trolley all the way to the hotel, where the driver dropped us off and continued on his way.

The three of us had a bus ride all the way from the Romanian border to our hotel in Budapest for a used three-dollar pen. The captain got the pen. The lieutenant got nothing. It was the cheapest trip we ever made.

The next trip, in 1976, I made with my wife and both David and Mordie. This time I drove myself. I got a car at the Budapest airport and drove to Viseu by way of Oradea. In Viseu, Mr. Friedman was still alive, but the synagogue had been torn down. Once again I could not find my grandmother's grave.

On that trip, Friedman gave me a Torah to take back. "No Judaism will endure here," he said. So he gave it to me, but the police took it away at the Hungarian border. The Romanians said it was part of their patrimony and, despite all my efforts, I have not been able to get it back. The motivation for claiming all that so-called patrimony really isn't to preserve anything; it is a way to obtain bribes, a way to extort money.

My wife, our two sons, and I took a long, beautiful drive north from Bucharest. The boys had a great time. In Sighet there was a man named Fuchs who made his living providing food for tourists. He lived in a large house and made home-cooked meals. I remember well our first meal there: chicken, mashed potatoes, chicken soup, and homemade bread. In general, Mordy did not like the food in Romania, but he liked what he had in Sighet.

We stayed in the same hotel that we had used on the trip in 1974, at the edge of the Tisa River just across the border from what is now Ukraine. It was night when we checked in. In the lobby was a bar with some very boisterous Romanians. Unlike Hungarians and Germans, Romanians are happy-go-lucky types; they are friendly; they invite you for a drink. Yours is mine, mine is yours. There is no big problem.

So we sat in the lobby next to the bar and everyone was having a good time. All of a sudden a guy came in and was acting like a manager, like a boss. I said to my wife that this man was not a guest. He was somebody.

I invited him to come over, and we tried talking in a few languages. Finally he spoke my language. I said to him in Yiddish, "You're the boss here, right?"

"What makes you think so?" he asked. "The government is the boss, I'm not."

"But," I insisted, "you must be involved here."

"Sure," he said.

I asked him what he did, and he finally admitted he was the hotel manager.

"Why are you here this late?" I asked. (It was 11:30 P.M.)

"You don't understand," he replied.

"That's why I'm asking questions," I said. "I don't understand."

The manager then pointed to the bartender. "Do you see that guy over there? He is selling whiskey. He steals money and I come to take my share, my cut."

Nothing changes, I thought.

"So how are you doing?" I asked. "How's business?"

"What do you mean business?" he said. "I work for the government."

"How's your life?" I continued.

"Everything's great," he said. "I have no problems. I do great and I have added insurance."

I asked him what his insurance was, and he said that his wife was a gentile, a Romanian. "In case something happens to the Jews," he said, "I have insurance. She is going to protect me."

When we came back on the next trip, he was gone. The government had continued to discharge Jews from key positions.

In the summer of 1995, on my fourth trip back to Viseu after having come to America, Edith and I were accompanied by Florence, David, Mordy, and their families. This time, my grandmother's grave was found. The discoverer was our granddaughter, Shoshana, who translated the Hebrew on one of the tombstones and found that it was the grave of her great-great-grandmother.

We wanted our grandchildren to be able to visit not only Viseu but also Papa, the town in Hungary where Edith once lived, and the Slovak Republic where her family can be traced back for almost two hundred years. All of us went to Bratislava, where the great Chasam Sofer lived and is buried. So it was that our grandchildren saw for themselves what had been Edith's and my part of the world in Hungary, Slovakia, and Romania.

Conclusion

I have called what I have written, "Letter To My Children." It has been directed to them because I want them to know what they lost in the Holocaust, not only in terms of family members but also in terms of a way of life that is gone forever.

I want them to know how people lived in my part of the world, how they were very happy spiritually while they struggled physically. By our standards in America they were poor people, but in reality they were very rich. For them what was paramount was their family life. This included the respect that a child had for parents, grandparents, and all communal leaders, the responsibility that parents and grandparents had for the children, and the total dedication of parents for their children's success.

But success did not mean worldly success. It meant providing a child with knowledge. That knowledge consisted of Jewish knowledge, religious knowledge, worldly knowledge, and a knowledge of ethics, the ethics of our fathers, forefathers, and leaders going back thousands of years.

This century has been the stormiest period of our history as Jews. Never before were millions killed in such a short time just because they were Jews, not by Nebuchadnezzar, not by Titus. No other people suffered losses of such magnitude and then recovered and reestablished lives in such a short time. The losses are incomprehensible. The reestablishment of our lives also is incomprehensible.

What happened and how it happened we will never understand. No matter how many books are written, we will never be able to understand. What we have to realize is that the human race is capable of all kinds of monstrosities. No suffering is so unimaginable that it cannot be inflicted by one human being on another. Yet how versatile and resilient the human spirit is! With hope and love for G-d and for human beings, we can overcome everything. Without them, we cannot.

Yet we can never forget the suffering that was inflicted by the German nation as a nation, not by a few Nazis, not by a few misguided people, but by the German nation. We can never forget that.

I have been asked if I will forgive. My answer has been and continues to be that I will forgive when I hear the Germans say, "We have caused all this suffering. We are guilty of all the killings. Please forgive us." I have never heard them say it. All I hear are excuses: "We did not know," "We did not do it," "We were good," and "Let us forget."

We cannot forget.

At the same time, we cannot belabor it so much that our psyches are damaged and we act irrationally. We have to act rationally. We have to act normally, humanely. We have to make sure that our roots, planted so many years ago, are nourished. The only way they can be nourished is by education—an education in history, in morals, in ethics, in our traditions.

That education must never take any form that causes intolerance of other people. We have to remember that in order to be human we have to behave humanely. To make certain that we follow this course, we have our traditions to guide us. We do not have to fall for any new, misguided ideas. Our forefathers taught us sufficiently how to behave, and we can never forget that.

The family and the responsibilities of family members to one another are foremost. We can never forget that.

The secret of our people's survival is our families. Going back hundreds, if not thousands, of years, Jewish families have been treasured. "Bilam said to the Jewish people, 'How good are your tents, Jacob, your dwellings, Israel,'" meaning the closeness of the families. Because of our family traditions, no matter how difficult times were, our survival was assured. Whenever family responsibility was overlooked or questioned and traditions abandoned, our people have lost their identity and sense of community.

I sometimes ask myself where would we be, what would have happened, if Hitler had never come? I do not know. Life probably would have gone on. I would probably be doing what my forefathers did. But I know for sure that many millions of our people and their descendants would be here.

Where we would be personally, I do not know. We can look back and learn from history, but we cannot go back and brood about it. We must look forward.

During my lifetime the world has changed greatly. It will never be the same. Our family has been very fortunate because we have spiritual values, material things, cohesiveness. Fortunately, our children and grandchildren are following in the footsteps of our forefathers.

I was fortunate to have a father who was with us until a few years ago. Few people of my generation, the survivors of the concentration camps, were so fortunate. Despite the suffering he went through in the First World War and during the atrocities of the Second, he lived a long life, saw the success of his three surviving children, and enjoyed his grandchildren. In fact, he was at the weddings of all of them. Most important, he never lost his faith and his hope. We always have to be thankful for that.

My wife and I are fortunate that we have been able to build many institutions of health and education in various parts of this country, Europe, and Israel. We are fortunate that we had sufficient sense to see that this happened while we were alive and able to enjoy the fruits of our labors. We hope to continue along those paths for many years to come.

My wife and I are fortunate that we emigrated to America, a country with a rich tradition of tolerance, a place that has allowed us to reestablish our lives materially and religiously. For this we always will be grateful to this great country, a country where one can ascend to heights limited only by one's ability and desire.

When the war ended, Edith and I were in a Europe that was in chaos. There was no food. For the surviving Jews there were almost no families—hardly one lived through it intact. There was no communal establishment. There was no religious establishment. There were no communal leaders. Moreover, in much of the continent there was no government. Nothing existed. It was total chaos.

A greater number of inmates of the camps died after liberation than ultimately survived. And yet, despite all this, survivors were able to spring back quickly. They reestablished communal help organizations and, more important, they started leaving for Israel and America. In America, at the end of the 1940s, Jewish religious life was increasingly more diluted by the trend of assimilation. There were few who could be described as scholars. Many had died. In 1945 and 1946, when the refugees began coming here, there was a revival of the Jewish communal religious establishment. I hate to think what would have happened to Jewry in America if there had been no influx of these religious people. The same thing happened in other parts of the world where religious refugees emigrated.

There was an order given by Hitler to one of his top officials in Poland to make certain that there was no migration of Jewish religious leaders from that country to other parts of the world, because they would keep the religion alive. Hitler's order was to annihilate both the Jews and their religion. He almost accomplished his objective. Nevertheless, some leaders survived, and they reestablished their religious leadership both in the United States and Israel.

If it had not been for that influx of religious people, the world of Judaism would be greatly different from what it is today. While we see a continuing assimilation of Jews into non-Jewish America, along with disintegration of family structures, more single-parent families, more divorces, more intermarriages, and more drifting away from religion, at the same time we see a great revival in Orthodox circles all over the country, in Chicago, New York, New Jersey, Florida—all over.

This is a highly significant revival. New educational institutions have been established and are bursting at the seams. Jewish children are better educated in their religion and are family oriented. I have great hope for future generations. The problem right now is the lack of sufficient money to build the educational institutions for all the children and older students who want to attend. More money is being spent, but even more is needed.

Never in Jewish history, not even in the great eras of Babylon and Spain, has there been such a multitude of highly educated religious people as we have now in America and in other parts of the world. In all walks of life, in all professions, there are highly talented men and women practicing their religion. Many of them are children of survivors. Their parents and grandparents came from the concentration camps and ghettos. This is a real source of pride. It also gives one reason to hope that our people will continue to be dedicated to our Jewish traditions.

I will never understand why my wife and I were saved while so many perished. We know that only a few out of the thousands of deportees were kept alive as slave laborers after we reached Auschwitz. The vast majority were taken straight to the gas chambers and murdered. Why this happened is for Someone higher to explain.

We cannot understand that. What we must understand, however, is the responsibility we bear to carry on our traditions and our way of life and not to succumb to the new winds that are blowing and tearing away so many of us from our roots. This places a serious burden on each of us, a great responsibility that may be the reason we who were there and still live were saved.

My wife and I are from the last generation and, when we are gone, there will be no one left who experienced the old traditions that were nurtured and practiced for so many hundreds of years. We have seen the traumatic change from near total annihilation to moments of triumph, from ashes to revival. Because of our children, grandchildren, and others of their generations, our hope for the future is strong. It is with this hope that I conclude my letter, my gift, to my children.